LANDSKIPPING

LANDSKIPPING

Painters, Ploughmen and Places

Anna Pavord

BLOOMSBURY

LONDON · OXFORD · NEW YORK · NEW DELHI · SYDNEY

Bloomsbury Publishing
An imprint of Bloomsbury Publishing Plc

50 Bedford Square   1385 Broadway
London   New York
WC1B 3DP   NY 10018
UK   USA

www.bloomsbury.com

British Library Cataloguing-in-Publication Data
A catalogue record for this book is available from the British Library.

Library of Congress Cataloguing-in-Publication data has been applied for.

ISBN: HB: 978-1-4088-6891-1
ePub: 978-1-4088-6894-2

2 4 6 8 10 9 7 5 3 1

Typeset by Newgen Knowledge Works (P) Ltd., Chennai, India
Printed and bound in Great Britain by CPI Group (UK) Ltd, Croydon CR0 4YY

To find out more about our authors and books visit www.bloomsbury.com.
Here you will find extracts, author interviews, details of forthcoming events and
the option to sign up for our newsletters.

Dedicated to the inheritors: Josh, Romilly, Raf, Zac and Ziggy Dale,
Maisie, Tom and Agnes Ringer, Jack, Fergus, Xan and
Hector Gathorne-Hardy

CONTENTS

PART THREE: PROSPECTS AND PLACE

LANDSKIPPING

Samuel Palmer, *Landscape, Girl Standing* (c. 1826)

Beginning

You wouldn't exactly call it a mountain. More of a hill. But where I grew up, in the border country between England and Wales, it was the tallest thing around, 1,200 ft and pointed, a distinctive triangle rising up on the backs of the Deri, the Rholben and the Llanwenarth Breast. To me, the Sugar Loaf was certainly a mountain. In fact, I thought it was a volcano, although my father in his clear, schoolmasterly way, explained several times why it could not be. It was very smooth, silhouetted against the sky. The scrub oaks that grew over the softer slopes of the three lower hills stopped as they came within sight of the Sugar Loaf. Too steep. For me as well as them.

But we often climbed it. Round the side of the Sugar Loaf, where the landscape opened out on to Forest Coalpit and the Black Mountains, there was a boggy place where globeflowers grew. There were kingcups everywhere along the streams of my uncles' farms, but the globeflower – paler, taller, more poised – was a rarity and we went every year to admire them, a kind of pilgrimage for my mother. She was a great botanist – in the old-fashioned way. She could name every different kind of grass in any field she walked through. She made a collection of them, pressed pale and bleached in a book of cartridge paper, with their names, common and botanical, written in white ink underneath.

She could name the owner, too, of almost every farm we looked out on to from the high sides of the Sugar Loaf. She'd been born in this landscape. So had my father. It was intimately known. We climbed up on to the flanks of the Sugar Loaf to gather winberries, always in the same china cups, too cracked to hold tea, but too pretty to throw away. The day before my geometry O level, my mother was waiting after school with a picnic in a basket and we climbed up through the beech trees of St Mary's Vale to a spring on the side of the Sugar Loaf where she tested me on my theorems. Pythagoras would stick better, she firmly believed, if it was taken in with a view.

So the square on the hypotenuse is inextricably mixed still with bracken, tall and green, the slightly damp acid smell of the turf always cropped short by the sheep on the hill and the view back down over the Deri and the Rholben to the Usk shining in the valley below. Beyond the river was the Blorenge, where we never went.

Partly this was a matter of geography. We lived just underneath the Deri, so naturally it was the landscape we were most often in, the one we knew best. We would have needed transport, which we did not have, to get over the river to the Blorenge. And it was a big, bare, forbidding hunk, with a dip in the flank that faced our house, where shadows gathered too early. There was another reason to stick to our side of the river. The Blorenge was a kind of gatekeeper to another country. Lying in bed at night, I could see from my window the great flares that lit up the sky from the furnaces of the iron masters, Guest, Keen and Nettlefold in Brynmawr and Blaenavon. Over there, the valleys which had once been green were bounded by grey-black heaps of slag. So, I suppose the fragility of a landscape was stitched into me from the beginning. And a need for land to go up and down if I'm to feel comfortable in it.

There were maps in our house, but they were for people staying with us. We never needed them because, though we had no notion of footpaths or other 'rights of way', we knew exactly how to get anywhere we wanted to go in the hills. Mostly we were roaming around without parents. Up the lane, through Angry Native's farmyard, up the steep pasture where we sometimes found mushrooms, over a couple of stiles, past the guinea fowl with their nervous 'Go back. Go back. Go back,' and into the scrub oak woods of the Deri, where every winter we built a kind of headquarters. The sides of these hills were littered with small quarries where stone had been carted down to build a cottage or a barn. It was not difficult to roof in one of these dugouts with branches cast from the scrub oaks and thatch them with bracken, brown and dry. The fronds would last all winter.

At the top of all three of the hills, the land flattened out and wide grass paths, kept open by the endless nibbling of sheep, led forward to the smooth cone of the mountain that was with us all our time out there on the hills. Not sublime. Not even as beautiful as other places I discovered later in life. But resilient. And deeply familiar. In hot summers, fires occasionally broke out in the dry whin and heather on the tops of the hills. Then we would burn fires of our own on top of the ash poles we carried, bracken and scrub stuffed inside sheep skulls (plenty of those on the hillsides) to make lanterns held high. We marched along the wide path on top of the Deri, six of us, in single file, our beacons aloft, with the wild fires burning either side of us. Celts against invading Romans. Welsh against English – none of it overtly expressed, but absorbed subliminally perhaps, because of the landscape in which we lived and the things which had happened there.

This was not – I see it now – a landscape to be given a capital L, the way the Landscape of Snowdonia in the north of Wales was. And the Lakes. Landscapes to be written about. Landscapes to be painted. William Gilpin scarcely gave the Sugar Loaf a glance, on his way west to Brecon from his famous journey down the Wye. The border country round Abergavenny is important to me because it is where I was born and brought up. Roots, if you are lucky enough to have them, still have an influence on the way you respond. That landscape, which I knew so closely, predisposed me to feel a connection with certain other landscapes later on. This isn't an unusual trait, this almost animal response to a new place. Do you feel comfortable here? Could you be sustained by this view?

What do we feel should be in a pleasing landscape? Sky, streams, rocks, trees are often assumed to be necessary components. I'd add hills. And pasture. The landscapes I prefer have an element of man's hand in them. Not too much, but enough to be able to add stone walls, plough and hedges to the view. And sheep. William Cobbett, on his travels through England in the 1820s, often mentions them. 'I like to look at the winding side of a great down,' he wrote, 'with two or three numerous flocks of sheep on it, belonging to different farms; and to see, lower down, the folds, in the fields, ready to receive them for the night.'[1] But everything depends on the balance of the two.

In Wasdale the tamed and the wild exist cheek by jowl. Here, in the Cumbria High Fells, is some of the toughest and most spectacular scenery in England, cursed by farmers, sighed over by poets and battered, since the whole concept of tourism was invented, by hordes of us visitors. I could never make the High Fells my home — that now lies in the soft, enclosing valleys of West Dorset — but it is where I go, like millions of others, to capture the sense of awe and splendour that only big mountains can give. North of Keswick you have Skiddaw and Blencathra. To the east of the Langdale Pikes is beautiful Helvellyn; to the west are Sca Fell and Pillar, a favourite with Edwardian members of the Fell and Rock Climbing Club, who photographed each other in splendid moustaches and boots, striking poses on the summit.

I am not one to see landscape as a series of things to be conquered: a river to be swum, a peak to be climbed, a cliff to be scaled, but Sca Fell attracts the conquering type. At 3,210 ft, it is the highest point in England. It is also a potent memorial, for in 1920 Lord Leconfield, its owner, gave it to the National Trust in memory of the men of the Lake District 'who fell for God and King, for freedom, peace and right in the Great War'. Four years later, the members of the Fell and Rock Climbing Club bought the land of twelve further Lakeland mountain tops, each more than 1,500 ft high, 3,000 acres in all, to commemorate (in an unusually fitting way) their dead comrades. A discreet but superbly lettered bronze tablet was unveiled on Great Gable on 8 June 1924:

> In glorious & happy memory of those whose names are inscribed below — members of this club — who died for their country in the European War 1914–1918, these fells were acquired by their fellow members & by them invested in The National Trust for the use & enjoyment of the people of our land for all time.

'If there is any communion with the spirits of dead warriors,' wrote W. T. Palmer, describing the event for the club's journal, 'surely they were very near that silent throng of climbers, hill-walkers and dalesfolk who assembled in soft rain and rolling mist on the high crest.'[2] Remember them when you look out over the glinting landscape of lake and tarn, scree and scrub that spreads out around you from Sca Fell's crest.

Did Neolithic man ever feel the urge to storm Sca Fell? He was close, fashioning axes on the slopes of Great Langdale from the Ordovician rock. Or did he stay sensibly on the lower contours, where later in the Dark Ages, farmers started the slow process of clearing and enclosing patches of land for their sheep and cattle? The small fields, with their stone wall buffers, represent survival in the harshest of environments. You see it nowhere more clearly than at Wasdale, a long thin valley where scree tumbles precipitously into the dark, enigmatic embrace of Wast Water.

The best thing about Wasdale is that it lies at the end of a No Through Road and once you have threaded your way in, there is little reason ever to get out. Its relative inaccessibility means that it has changed far less than other more-visited parts of the Lakes. Electricity only came here in the late 1970s. The road through it eventually bumps its nose into the fell at the end, conveniently close to the door of the Wasdale Head Inn. Yewbarrow sits humpily to the left. Black Sail Pass stretches ahead and Sca Fell beetles over the brow of the fell on the right.

But, if you are not the look-at-me-on-the-top-of this-rock type, you can forget poor, exhausted, emasculated Sca Fell and make instead for Illigill Head, where you can spread-eagle yourself in bracken and whin, a mere two thousand feet above sea level. Here you can cruise, like a glider, watching the pattern of peaks and fells, tarns and rivers rearrange themselves as you swing round the crescent of the fell ridge. Often, particularly in autumn, when views seem curiously suspended in time, the lake is so still it throws back a perfect mirror image of fell and rock, scree and sky. Shadows, Brobdingnagian in the morning light, scud across the landscape or lie in silhouette on the other side of the valley. The sky may be startlingly blue, but then from nowhere, weird heavy clouds will pull themselves together to drape heavily over the shoulders of Great Gable.

From the saddle of land above Fence Wood land drops on one side over fans of rough scree into Wast Water. On the other side, views stretch to Eskdale and beyond that, the sea, gleaming hazily around Seascale. Between the high peaks, the saddles are made from heath and mire, peat and acid grassland. In patches of soggy moss you can find huge colonies of sundew, one of the few carnivorous plants native to Britain. It hugs the ground, a rosette of small, reddish, spoon-shaped leaves which bristle with hairs, each tipped with a drop of fluid. Insects land on the plant, stick to the hairs and are doomed. The leaf closes in on itself and the flies are dissolved in the sundew's home-made soup.

You can drop off the top of the fell alongside Pickle Coppice, typical of the sparse plantations of evergreens that hang on to the sides of the slopes. In the valley bottoms, deciduous trees predominate: ash, alder, sycamore. When it has been raining, the sides of the hills here splinter into small streams, charging through moss and ferns to empty themselves in the River Mite below. Once in the valley, you can turn back up the hill, climbing between two narrow flanks of forestry plantation to come out on Tongue Moor, easy walking among rough-coated Herdwick sheep. Burnmoor Tarn, black and treeless, lies on the right, Sca Fell beyond it. By teatime you will be back on the saddle below Illigill, and by six o'clock you will be taking your boots off at the inn, which at dusk shines like a beacon at Wasdale Head.

The flat land of the valley head (and there is not much of it) is divided into a jigsaw of tiny, irregular fields, bounded by thick boulder stone walls. W. G. Hoskins, the grandfather of English landscape history, describes it as a medieval landscape. The National Trust, who own more than 30,000 acres of land in this area, date it to the sixteenth century. Whenever it was, it represents hard labour and thin pickings. But viewed, say, from the windy flanks of Pillar on a bad day, the valley, with its pattern of bright green fields and silver river, looks like Nirvana. To reach Pillar from Wasdale, you may take the Black Sail Pass, now an unfortunate motorway of a trail, then strike off to the left, past the Looking Stead on to the switchback of rocky mounds beyond. If the sun is still shining and the sky is still blue, the bulk of Yewbarrow will be cutting Wast Water into two shining halves with the gleaming disc of Burnmoor Tarn above it. But often on the final scramble to Pillar, when you are at close on 3,000 ft, a wind strikes, a vicious, malevolent, exhausting wind. With every step, you battle for balance like a novice tightrope walker. The High Fells show their cruel side and, like an animal, you crawl into the lee of a sheltering rock.

The weather, which we are used to dominating, needs to be taken seriously up here. The wind can pick you up from the ground and drop you in places you'd rather not be. Windy Gap, lower down, presents a potential escape route. You either keep to the high ground and get down gradually by way of Red Pike, or shoot down the near vertical scree run on the left to shorten the circuit and get out of the wind. The instant exit leaves you slipping and swearing down a half-mile chute until it drops you on the rocky grassland of Mosedale, where the sheepfolds wait, refuge incarnate.

Every October, a Shepherd's Meet is held in Wasdale. For more than a thousand years, sheep have sculpted this landscape. At the Meet, gimmers and rams bulge between makeshift hurdles, their fleeces dressed with reddle. As more and more sheep pass through their hands, the shepherds become covered in it too, trousers and jackets gathering the same red-brown ochre tints as the fleeces. The best Herdwick sheep are brought to the show. So are the best fell hounds, to race an extraordinary ten-mile circuit round the fells of Wasdale: up Mosedale, round Yewbarrow, back by Lingmell and Burnthwaite. The dogs are probably the ugliest you will ever see, like rangy foxhounds with narrow heads and tails, big feet and intelligent eyes.

Hounds are slipped in one of the small walled fields, close to the church. The owners crouch in a jumble, the dogs straining between their legs, held back by the folds of loose skin at their necks. As the starter's handkerchief goes down, the hounds streak away down the field, following a trail laid beforehand by a fell runner dragging a scent-soaked bundle of rags. The hounds jump six-foot stone walls like steeplechasers before disappearing in the bracken of the fell.

For the next tense half hour you will only catch glimpses of them, way up on the hills, streaming in a line along the scent, hurtling across streams, flying over boulders, indistinguishable to the naked eye. But when they come into view over the last mile, the hounds' owners race to the finishing line blowing whistles, screaming their dogs' names, waving big handkerchiefs in the air, banging feed dishes. The hounds clear the final wall amid a wild cacophony of cheering and banging and whistling and hurl themselves, molten bundles of off-white and brown, into the arms of their owners. A spectacle as intense and moving as this could only be set in the wild, tough landscape of the Cumbrian Fells.

PART ONE

PROSPECTS AND PAINTERS

Pray have you Rocks and Waterfalls?
For I am as fond of Landskip as ever

Letter (1768) from Thomas Gainsborough in Bath
to James Unwin in Derbyshire

Burrowdale, Cumberland from *The Beauties of England and Wales*, Vol. III,
by John Britton and Edward Wedlake Brayley (London, 1802)

CHAPTER I

Looking at the Lakes

THE LAKES HAVE never lost their ability to attract. In the eighteenth century it was one of the first places in Britain where people went for no other purpose than to look at the view. 'It is only within a few years', wrote Joseph Warton in 1756, 'that the picturesque scenes of our own country, our lakes, mountains, cascades, caverns and castles, have been visited and described.'[1] The Lakes, The Highlands, Snowdonia. Those were the three must-dos for those who travelled for pleasure in the eighteenth century. A 'correct' taste in landscape was now an accomplishment to be learned, as you might learn the piano. Or Greek. Was this view sublime? Or was it merely beautiful? Travellers then would have read Edmund Burke's essay, his *Philosophical Enquiry* published in 1757, and absorbed his distinctions. 'The sublime and beautiful are built on principles very different,' he wrote, 'and . . . their affections are as different: the great has terror for its basis; which, when it is modified, causes that emotion in the mind, which I have called astonishment; the beautiful is founded on more positive pleasure, and excites in the soul that feeling, which is called love.'[2] They would also have read James Thomson's poem *The Seasons*, extolling the beauties of nature and landscape.

The Lakes, with its craggy peaks and aweful screes, its rushing waterfalls and its precipices, could do terror rather well. And you could shiver in a pleasurable way, knowing that, at any moment, you could abandon the sublime and embrace instead a warm fire and a hot dinner at one of the many inns that made a seasonal living from landscape tourists. Crowning all the aesthetic imperatives to come to this place was the practical fact that a tourist, starting, as was often the case, in the south of England, could actually get to Cumberland and Westmorland by road. Between 1760 and 1774, 452 separate turnpike trusts were set up. Another 643 were incorporated between 1785 and the end of the century. By the middle of the nineteenth century there were plans to bring in tourists by train, prompting Wordsworth, in December 1844, to fire off an angry letter to the editor of the *Morning Post*, condemning the 'intrusion of a railway with its scarifications, its intersections, its noisy machinery, its smoke, and swarms of pleasure-hunters, most of them thinking that they do not fly fast enough through the country which they have come to see'.

'We have too much hurrying about in these islands,' he concluded, 'much for idle pleasure, and more from over activity in the pursuit of wealth, without regard to the good or happiness of others.'[3] Commenting on the letter, the *Spectator* magazine thought that Wordsworth would do better to stick to poetry. There was an unpleasant air of what we might now call nimbyism about the letter, and an even more unpleasant assumption that railways would bring the wrong kind of people, ill-equipped to appreciate the beauty of the place. 'Wordsworth thinks there ought to be preserves of poets, as there are of partridges; and that Cumberland is equally suited for sheep-runs and poet-runs. The expiring breed of Lake poets ought especially to be kept up.'[4]

But long before the arrival of the railways, early visitors had published accounts of their travels to see the landscapes of the Lake District, personal memoirs of particular journeys, such as William Hutchinson's *An Excursion to the Lakes in Westmoreland*

and Cumberland, August 1773 (London, 1774). And even then
Hutchinson noted how often the landscape tourist, having just
arrived at a destination, seemed anxious to be moving on to
the next: 'As a gentleman said to Robin Partridge the day after
we were upon Windermere, "Good God! how delightful! –
how charming! – I could live here for ever! – Row on, row
on, row on, row on"; and after passing one hour of exclama-
tions upon the Lake, and half an hour at Ambleside, he ordered
his horses into his phaeton, and flew off to take (I doubt not)
an equally *flying* view of Derwent water.' Hutchinson noticed
too how the natural wonders of the place were being gradually
overtaken by the man-made. He describes, for instance, the
boat fitted out by the Earl of Surrey with twelve brass cannon,
fired off to give the Earl and his guests the pleasure of listening
to the echoes:

> The sound of every distant water-fall was heard, but for an
> instant only; for the momentary stillness was interrupted
> by returning echo on the hills behind us; where the report
> was repeated like a peal of thunder bursting over our heads,
> continuing for several seconds, flying from haunt to haunt,
> till once more the sound gradually declined; – again the voice
> of water-falls possessed the interval.[5]

Cannons and their echoes proved to be very popular attractions for the tourists. The landlord of the Lodore Inn at
Derwentwater offered two: one cost 4/6 a firing, the other
2/6. But only the noisiest would do; the smaller cannon with
its cheaper echo rusted away for lack of use.[6]

The influx of tourists to the Lakes also created a new and very
lucrative kind of publishing venture – the guidebook. Thomas
West's *A Guide to the Lakes, in Cumberland, Westmorland, and
Lancashire* was the first book aimed primarily at tourists, listing

the main attractions and the best way to see them. It appeared
in 1778 and by 1812 was in its tenth edition. Like the *Rough
Guides* of today they were useful aids for people who wanted
to tick off the Things To Do without wasting too much time
looking for them. West listed the places, the 'stations' where
you got the best (that is to say the most generally approved)
views of the lakes. To avoid any mistakes (the horror – you had
been to Grasmere and taken in the wrong view), crosses were
cut into the turf at various points, so that there could be no
doubt in the minds of the landscape tourists where they ought
to stand. At the most popular (the most easily reached) points,
the 'stations' turned into shelters, because quite a lot of the
awefulness of the Lake District depended on storms sweeping
down from the heights. At each point, West's guide listed the
landmarks to be noted, the views to be taken in.

The second edition of West's *Guide* (1780) included an
interesting appendix: the journal kept by the poet Thomas
Gray on his tour of the Lake District in 1769. Gray was a
pioneer in his appreciation of the Lakes landscape and at the
time that he was travelling, views had not yet been codified. A
few viewpoints, though, such as the one by the ferry landing
on Windermere's western shore, had already become established favourites, and West described how from this point 'a
glorious sheet of water expands itself to the right and left,
in curves bearing from the eye; bounded on the west by the
continuation of the mountain where you stand.'[7] Gray put on
a blindfold for the ferry crossing from Bowness, and, arriving
at the landing, turned his back to the famous landscape and
looked at it first through the lens of his Claude glass. The view
did not properly exist until it had been mediated.

Today's tourists often do the same kind of thing. It seems
to be the photograph of a landscape that tells them they have
seen it, not the landscape itself. The Claude glass, though, a

four-inch convex mirror mounted on black foil, did more than
an iPhone. It 'corrected' the landscape, made it more manage-
able, more painterly, got rid of extraneous detail. By using a
special glass tinted in a bluish-grey, the tourist could turn a
sunlit view into a moonlit one. There was a yellow 'sunrise'
glass too, for those who couldn't be bothered to get up to see
the real thing. But using one could be a hazardous business,
because you had to keep your back to the view. In a letter to
the poet Joseph Warton, Gray described how he 'fell down on
my back across a dirty lane with my glass open in one hand,
but broke only my knuckles: stay'd nevertheless, & saw the
sun set in all its glory'.[8]

The great poet of the Lakes was, of course, William
Wordsworth, who wrote a tart poem 'On Seeing some Tourists
of the Lakes pass by reading, a practise very common'. He
intended to include it in his *Poems in Two Volumes* (1807) but
withdrew it, perhaps because he had already decided to give
those tourists a guide of his own to read. Was he, as the Grand
Old Man of the Lakes, irritated by West's success? Anony-
mously, he wrote the commentary to Joseph Wilkinson's *Select
Views in Cumberland, Westmorland and Lancashire*, published in
1810. Twelve years later, he threw off the anonymity and had
the text reprinted separately as *A Description of the Lakes in the
North of England*.

Ruskin described Wordsworth as a painter in poetry, but
in his greatest work Wordsworth went far beyond the topographical exactness of early poems such as 'An Evening Walk'
(1787) with its 'huddling rill' and 'moss of darkest green'. In
later works such as *The Prelude*, the outward, physical landscape (the poet is sitting above Esthwaite Water to the west of
Windermere) becomes the catalyst to explore a more complex
landscape of the mind. He gave up 'pampering myself with
meagre novelties/Of colour and proportion'.[9] Focus shifts

from the object seen to the subject who is seeing. 'The mind', wrote Wordsworth in an essay on the Sublime, 'tries to grasp at something towards which it can make approaches but which it is incapable of attaining.'

Inevitably, as his poems gathered wider and wider acclaim, Wordsworth himself became an object of pilgrimage. On a journey north with his friend Charles Brown, Keats, then just twenty-three years old, determined to visit the poet. Writing to his brother Tom from Ambleside in the Lake District (27 June 1818) he describes the occasion:

> We arose this morning at six, because we call it a day of rest, having to call on Wordsworth who lives only two miles hence – before breakfast we went to see the Ambleside water-fall. The morning beautiful – the walk easy among the hills. We, I may say, fortunately, missed the direct path, and after wandering a little found it out by the noise – for, mark you, it is buried in trees, in the bottom of the valley – the stream itself is interesting throughout with 'mazy error over pendant shades' [he was quoting Milton's *Paradise Lost*]. Milton meant a smooth river – this is buffeting all the way on a rocky bed ever various – but the waterfall itself, which I came suddenly upon, gave me a pleasant twinge. First we stood a little below the head about half way down the first fall, buried deep in trees, and saw it streaming down two more descents to the depth of near fifty feet – then we went in a jut of rock nearly level with the second fall-head – where the first fall was above us, and the third below our feet still – at the same time we saw that the water was divided by a sort of cataract island on whose other side burst out a glorious stream – then the thunder and the freshness. At the same time the differ-ent falls have as different characters; the first darting down the slate-rock like an arrow; the second spreading out like a

fan – the third dashed into a mist – and the one on the other side of the rock a sort of mixture of all these. We afterwards moved away a space, and saw nearly the whole, more mild, streaming silverly through the trees. What astonishes me more than any thing is the tone, the coloring, the slate, the stone, the moss, the rock-weed . . .'[10]

Wordsworth was out. But Keats had had the waterfall. And we have the letter, fighting (brilliantly) to set down what he'd seen, this restless mass of the waterfall, endlessly recreating itself even as he was trying to capture it. This is why you can with pleasure come back and back and back to a landscape; it is never the same. It is at the same time unchanging and ephemeral, timeless yet particular. Sometimes, above Caldbeck, looking down into the valley, the mist is so thick that it spreads over the land like one of the lakes. Perception of what is real and what is solid disappears. You know, because you've been there before, that this isn't a lake, but if you hadn't, it could be. A huge lake with amorphous grey shapes emerging from its edges and rooks weaving black threads in and out of the grey. Rivulets of mist may be oozing through the valley to join up with clouds in the sky. Driving into this landscape is like diving into the lake itself because all the land is gone. You are swimming in a deep, enveloping caesura, the trees appearing like great underwater creatures, suspended in the mist.

Or, from the windows of the chapel in Caldbeck ('Remember NOW thy Creator' 1832) you can look out on the landscape, framed like a series of paintings: sycamores, stunted maybe, but surviving, stone walls fused and sinuous. Grey. In the foreground, gorse bushes slung with hammocks of spider-web.

Or, by chance, you may find the Aira Force, north of Ullswater, and watch the river plaiting its way widely over rocks of blue and buff and grey. Then suddenly, unexpectedly, the whole leisurely bulk of the river is penned between jutting cliffs of rock on either side, wet with spray, green with moss. Squeezed into this narrow passage it then has to fall, to become part of the contained, boiling cauldron of water below. Smoky spume rises from the turmoil and drifts on downstream, through alder, birch and oak with small, stiff polypody ferns growing along their branches. Away from the damp, rushy smell of the river, the acrid smell of fox hangs in the air. And below is Ullswater, the water of the lake sometimes so calm and still that it could be a hole, a great black hole reflecting back the landscape.

The shape-changing quality of the Lakes landscapes, mist drifting into sky, water mirroring land, struck all who visited it. The poet Robert Southey was typical of the many visitors who struggled to describe what they were seeing: 'It was a bright evening,' he wrote,

the sun shining, and a few white clouds hanging motionless in the sky. There was not a breath of air stirring, not a wave, a ripple or wrinkle on the lake, so that it became like a great mirror, and represented the shires, mountains, sky and clouds so vividly that there was not the slightest appearance of water. The great mountain-opening being reversed in the shadow became a huge arch, and through that magnificent portal the long vale was seen between mountains and bounded by mountain beyond mountain, all this in the water, the distance perfect as in the actual scene – the single houses standing far up in the vale, the smoke from their chimneys – everything the same, the shadow and the substances joining at their bases, so that it was impossible to distinguish where the reality ended and the image began. As we stood on the shore, heaven and the clouds and the sun seemed lying under us; we were looking down into a sky, as heavenly and beautiful as that overhead, and the range of mountains, having one line of summit under our feet and another above us, were suspended between two firmaments.[11]

Coleridge, visiting the Lakes for the first time in 1799, scribbled rough maps in his notebook, showing how the lakes related to each other, marking in the main towns and dotting in the few routes that connected them. Describing Ullswater, he employs an almost painterly, pointilliste technique to try and evoke the changing effects of sunlight on the scene:

A little below Placefell a large Slice of calm silver – above this a bright ruffledness, or atomic sportiveness – motes in the sun? – Vortices of flies? – how shall I express the Banks waters all fused Silver, that House too its slates rainwet silver in the sun, & its shadows running down in the water like a column . . . the two island Rocks in the Lake . . . the one scarce visible in the shadow-coloured Slip now bordered by the melted Silver – the one nearer to me, likewise in the glossy shadow . . . How the scene changes – What tongues of Light shoot out from the Banks . . .[12]

Compare Coleridge's tumble of words with Francis Towne's cool assemblage of superimposed triangles in the watercolour he made of Rydal Water, or the stencil-like fixedness of his *View at Ambleside*, both made in 1786.[13] The painter had no option but to distil, to capture one moment, even as it was changing before their eyes. In its first use, after all, landscape was a word made for painters, not writers.

Paul Sandby, *Snowdon in Carnarvonshire*, engraved
by William Walker (1779)

CHAPTER 2

Painting the Prospect

WHEN IT FIRST appeared, 'landscape' was considered a foreign word, often written the Dutch way – *landschap* – and used to describe the pictures that artists in England began to make in the eighteenth century. It's odd that it didn't happen before, England being such a small country with such variety in its natural scenery. But nobody asked for it. Painters made their livings from portraits and history paintings. Thomas Blount, in 1656, described landscape in a painting as 'an expressing of the Land, by Hills, Woods, Castles, Valleys, Rivers, Cities, &c, as far as may be shewed in our Horizon. All that which in a Picture is not of the body or argument thereof is Landskip, Parergon, or by-work.'[1] Only later, as the eighteenth century progressed, did it take on the sense in which we use it now: 'A view or prospect of natural inland scenery, such as can be taken in at a glance from one point of view; a piece of country scenery.'[2] By the late nineteenth century another subtle shift had taken place. Now the word could also be used to define 'a tract of land with its distinguishing characteristics and features, esp. considered as a product of modifying or shaping processes and agents (usually natural)'.[3] The first was a personal matter, the second a product of geology and meteorology.

From the beginning, artists had a problem with the landscapes they painted in that most of those who looked at them felt they should work like portraits and give a likeness, as exact as possible, of the scene the artist had chosen to represent. Richard Wilson (1713/14–82), reckoned by many to be the founder of the British school of landscape painting, had spent the years between 1750 and c.1757 working in Italy, and a reviewer in the *Sun* (July 1814) evidently felt he had brought too much of the place home with him. 'Many of his landscapes of English views are not congenial to the soil and climate of England,' he wrote. 'They partake too much of southern skies, and lose the character which ought to belong to them, to acquire that of another quarter of the globe.'[4] When Wilson died, wrote Henry Fuseli, he was at least 'relieved from the apathy of cognoscenti, the envy of rivals, and the neglect of a tasteless public'.[5] After him, the deluge: Thomas Gainsborough, Paul Sandby, Alexander Cozens, John Cozens, Thomas Jones, Joseph Mallord William Turner, John Constable – all born in the fifty years between 1727 and 1777. By 1810, landscapes had come to dominate the art scene.

Gainsborough (1727–88), who like Wilson had started his career as a portrait painter, began his experiments in landscape with models set up in his studio. Arranged according to prevailing aesthetic theory, these might be made from bits of coal and cork with mirror for water and florets of broccoli for trees. While living in Bath, reported Prince Hoare, he became 'so disgusted at the blind preference paid to his powers of portraiture, that for many years . . . he regularly shut up all his landscapes in the back apartments of his house, to which no common visitors were admitted'.[6] There was so little call for his landscapes that he gave away his oil painting, *The Harvest Wagon*,[7] with its feathery trees and rowdy party of haymakers, in exchange for a grey horse belonging to a local carrier, Walter Wiltshire, who regularly drove Gainsborough's pictures from Bath up to London for exhibitions.

Gainsborough had been a great fan of the 1779 Drury Lane pantomime *The Wonders of Derbyshire*, with scenery painted by his friend, Philip de Loutherbourg (1740–1812). The Cavern of Castleton, Eden Hole, Mam Tor, Poole's Hole, Tideswell – wonder followed wonder in this extraordinary show in which the Derbyshire landscape, suitably sublimated, was the star, the plot, the entire raison d'être of the production. De Loutherbourg got £500 a year as stage designer at the Drury Lane, where he worked for eight years, first with the actor-manager, David Garrick, then with Sheridan. When he left, in 1781, he set up his own miniature theatre, the Eidophusikon, and continued to experiment with ways of giving to an audience all the ooh-aah of the wilder landscapes of England without their having to leave the conveniences of the capital.

Essentially a metropolitan man, Gainsborough was one of those who enjoyed de Loutherberg's Derbyshire without getting his feet wet. Yet in 1783 even he succumbed to the lure of landscape, telling his friend William Pearce, chief clerk of the Admiralty, that he was planning a trip to Cumberland and Westmorland and hoped 'to mount all the Lakes at the next Exhibition, in the great stile'.[8] He got there in the summer of that year, but his Lake District pictures did not hang in the Academy's exhibition. Gainsborough quarrelled violently with the Academicians and instead showed the pictures at his home, Schomberg House on the south side of Pall Mall in London.

By 1783, when Gainsborough went off to the Lakes, the notion of going to a particular landscape with the idea of it inspiring a body of work was well established. But in 1771, when the painter, Paul Sandby, set off on a tour of North Wales – then described as 'the fag end of Creation' – it was still an adventure. Sandby travelled with his patron, Sir Watkin Williams-Wynn of Wynnstay Park, near Chirk, one of the richest men in Wales.[9] The journey lasted two weeks and took Sir Watkin and Sandby from Llangollen to Bala, Dolgelly, Harlech, Carnarvon and Bangor, returning to Wynnstay by way of the turnpike road to Conwy and Holywell. Sir Watkin's agent, Samuel Sidebotham, kept meticulous records, showing the party included '5 Gentlemen 9 servants and 13 horses', and cost £111 7s 6d (nearly £12,000 in today's money). It was Sidebotham who, at Gwerclas on 22 August, paid the 'Boy that held the Horses at the Waterfall', who, on the 29th at Llanberis, paid 'the Guide to the Mountain'. Sidebotham sorted out the bills at the inns and the fees due on the turn-pike roads from Bangor to Conway and from St Asaph to Holywell.

Still, in the context of the time, this was a pioneering jour-ney and Sandby's *XII Views*, published in 1776 as a series of aquatints, introduced the public to a landscape far less famil-iar than the Lakes. Thomas Pennant had not yet published his *Tour in Wales*. The Whig topographer and author Henry Penruddocke Wyndham had not, at this time, brought out accounts of either of his Welsh journeys (he travelled during the summers of 1774 and 1777). The accepted itinerary – Chirk, Llangollen, through the Vale of Clwyd, Conway and Carnarvon for their castles, Snowdon and beautiful Cader Idris, Aberystwyth and inland to Hafod – had not yet worn its ruts into the rough roads of North Wales.

So, the leisured classes of Britain, for whom 'looking over prints' was such an amiable way to pass a wet Sunday after-noon, could shiver agreeably at the sublime grandeur of the 'Great Mountain Snowdon' which Sandby included as No. 10 of his *Views*. They could thrill to the articulated thunder of the River Conway as it poured over the rocks supporting the Pont-y-Pair (No. 12 in the series) where the carrier's cart provides the scale to set in context the huge, jagged range of mountains beyond.

On the title page, Sandby describes his *XII Views in North Wales* as 'part of a tour through that fertile and romantick country'. He does not include the word 'sublime', and perhaps Burke would allow only two of the twelve aquatints (the ones of Snowdon and the Pont-y-Pair bridge) to fit into his tightly defined parameters of sublimity. Vastness was one of Burke's criteria, and the aquatint Sandby made of The Great Mountain accentuates the overpowering scale of the landscape with the little boat set in the foreground on Llanberis Lake. (Sidebotham, a counterpoint to the sublime if ever there was one, included the fee for the boatman in his accounts.) Clouds drift over the shoulder of the peak itself and the deep fissures worn in its flanks by winter spates suggest the slow sculpting by wind and weather that has produced this overwhelming scene.

English landscape tourists had rather an idealised view of Wales, particularly the wild, rocky more inaccessible north of the country. Here, they thought, was a people and a country with a romantic past, and a culture undiluted by intruders, where harpers still harped and bards barded. Here were the true descendants of the mythical Ancient Britons, pushed ever westwards by waves of invaders on English shores. It wasn't strictly true but it didn't matter. Thomas Gray's poem 'The Bard' (1757) had a rapturous success, retelling the story of Edward I's massacre of Wales's poets. The last bard, theatrically positioned on a rock high above the river Conway, hurls curses at the Normans before throwing himself into the raging water below.

Sandby made a painting of the scene, which, like the poem, attracted a lot of exclamation marks. 'Such a picture!' wrote William Mason to Lord Nuneham, having in 1760 seen 'An Historical Landskip, representing the Welsh Bard, in the opening of Mr Gray's celebrated ode'. 'Such a Bard! Such a headlong

flood! Such a Snowdon! Such giant oaks! Such desert caves!'[10]
This was the time when looking at landscape, whether it was
the real thing, or transmuted into art, became the hallmark of
a cultivated person. But you had to be able to recognise when
a foreground was 'good' or when a background was lacking.
Landscape was a serious business; you weren't allowed, as we
do now, to amble through a mountain pass and say 'Wow.' You
had to be able to justify and dissect the wow, and here Edmund
Burke and, a little later, William Gilpin, were the presiding
authorities.

Burke, in his essay, *A Philosophical Enquiry into the Origin of
our Ideas of the Sublime and the Beautiful*, published in London in
1757, had described 'Beautiful' things as smooth, un-sudden
in their gradations, giving rise to pleasing emotions. To the
'Sublime', he gave qualities such as obscurity as well as vastness and the capacity to invite terror. 'A mode of terror or of
pain, is always the cause of the sublime.' A cloudy sky was more
sublime than a blue one, night 'more sublime and solemn' than
day. 'Sad and fuscous colours' such as black, brown and deep
purple heightened a sense of the sublime in a way that white,
green, yellow and blue could not. Whatever acts 'in conformity
to our will,' he wrote, 'can never be sublime'.[11] James Usher,
writing in *Clio; or a discourse on taste* (London, 1769) finds the
sublime in

> an ocean disturbed and agitated in storms; or a forest roar-
> ing, and bending under the force of the tempest. We are
> struck by it with more calmness, but equal grandeur, in the
> starry heavens: the silence, the unmeasured distance, and
> the unknown power united in that prospect, render it very
> awful in the deepest serenity. Thunder, with broken bursts
> of lightning through black clouds; the view of a cataract,
> whose billows fling themselves down with eternal rage; or

the unceasing sound of falling waters by night; the howling of animals in the dark: all these produce the sublime, by the association of the idea of invisible immense power.[12]

The picturesque was altogether cosier. Gilpin, who introduced the concept, defined it as 'that peculiar kind of beauty, which is agreeable in a picture'.[13] But whereas Burke's beauty was defined by smoothness, Gilpin's embraced a certain roughness and irregularity. In his *Three Essays: On Picturesque Beauty; On Picturesque Travel; and On Sketching Landscape* (London, 1792), he includes two plates. One shows three smooth interlocking hills; the other shows the same hills, given the prescribed Gilpin treatment: roughed up, irregularised, a tree silhouetted on the foremost hill, more indeterminate shrubbery on the left, a small precipice cut into the side of the right-hand hill, a track and two figures winding through the centre of the scene. 'It is the intention of these two prints to illustrate how very adverse the idea of *smoothness* is to the *composition* of landscape,' he explained, using italics in the way that we might use a marker pen. 'In the second of them the *great lines* of the landscape are exactly the same as in the first; only they are *more broken*.'[14]

Gilpin, who was vicar of Boldre in Hampshire, made his name with a series of *Observations* on the scenery of Britain published in 1782–1809, when travelling with the purpose of looking at views had become the fashionable rage among the well-to-do. His first tour took him to the River Wye, which he visited in 1770, and it was here that he worked out his criteria for the picturesque. Gilpin and his party began their journey down the Wye at Ross, Gilpin filling the notebook he kept during the tour[15] with sketches and descriptions of the landscape as they passed. Ross, Gilpin allowed, was 'sweetly situated', standing high above the river and commanding a 'distant prospect'. It was generally held that the best views were to be had from the churchyard at Ross, and from here Gilpin made a sketch of the river, curving in an elegant smooth loop in the foreground, dark scribbles of trees in the mid-ground. 'It is very beautiful,' he wrote, but later the beautiful was crossed out, to be replaced with a cooler adjective, 'amusing'. An amusing view but not 'correctly picturesque'. His objection was that it contained too many different elements; it was too broken up. He couldn't see how to rearrange the various components into a more 'correct' relationship with each other. Gilpin was not so much concerned with describing how landscapes actually looked as in judging whether they fitted his principles. They rarely did.

His *Observations on the River Wye* set the tone for all his succeeding books. He included few facts, little history, showed little interest in the lives of local people. He was an observant traveller but the view was all, and he was fantastically prescriptive in what made a good one. 'If nature gets wrong, I cannot help putting her right,' he explained cheerfully to his friend, the poet William Mason.[16] In his account of the Wye tour (it was published twelve years after the actual journey) he made clear that this was not a topographical guide, as Thomas West's *Guide to the Lakes* was, but an introduction to a particular way of seeing. The first edition of 700 copies sold well, but Gilpin's readers did not always grasp the difference between his intentions and the aim of a more regular guide. And Gilpin never understood why his fans, following in his footsteps, complained that the views which he had published so prettily in his book did not match the views that they were presented with on the river.

'As a drawer of existing scenes you are held as the greatest of *infidels*,' wrote Mason to Gilpin. 'If a Voyager down the river Wye takes out your Book, his very Boatman crys out,

"Nay, Sr, you may look in vain there. No body can find one Picture in it the least like."' Gilpin was unrepentant. Replying to Mason, he pointed out that he'd made his intentions clear from the start. This was a manual of aesthetics that happened to be focused on one particularly rewarding stretch of land-scape. 'I did all I could to make people believe they were *general ideas*, or *illustrations*, or any thing, but what they would have them to be, exact portraits; which I had neither time to make, nor opportunity, nor perhaps ability.' My sympathies are with the boatmen, struggling with the swift currents of the river and against the suspicions of their passengers, who would always assume that it was the boatman's fault that they were not seeing the famous view of Goodrich Castle from the 'correct' point.

Gilpin did all he could to set the book in the context he intended. In his introduction, as on the title page, he explains that, 'The following little work proposes a new object of pursuit; that of examining the face of a country *by the rules of picturesque beauty* . . . . Observations of this kind, through the vehicle of description,' he continues, 'have the better chance of being founded in truth; as they are not the offspring of theory; but are taken immediately from the scenes of nature, as they arise.' For Gilpin, the beauty of the Wye landscape arose from two circumstances: 'the *lofty banks* of the river, and its *mazy course*'. But every view on a river, however mazy its course, could be broken down into four components: 'the *area*, which is the river itself; the *two side-screens*, which are the opposite banks, and mark the perspective; and the *front-screen*, which points out the winding of the river.' He explains carefully how all the variations in the views that open up as the party moves downstream are brought about by 'the *contrast of the screens*. Sometimes one of the side-screens is elevated; sometimes the other; and sometimes the front. Or both the side-screens may

be lofty, and the front either high, or low.' Another four categories dealt with what he called the '*ornaments*' of the Wye:
ground, wood, rocks and buildings.[17]

In the circumstances a little judicious tweaking could be
sanctioned. 'Nature', Gilpin allowed, 'is always great in design.
She is an admirable colourist also; and harmonizes tints with
infinite variety, and beauty. But she is seldom so correct in
composition, as to produce a harmonious whole. Either the
foreground, or the background is disproportioned: or some
awkward line runs across the piece: or a tree is ill placed: or
a bank is formal: or something or other is not exactly what it
should be.'[18]

A rock, he explained, could be more important than it
might seem: 'Tint it with mosses, and lychens of various
hues, and you give it a degree of beauty. Adorn it with shrubs
and hanging herbage, and you still make it more picturesque.
Connect it with wood, and water, and broken ground; and
you make it in the highest degree interesting. It's colour, and
it's form are so accommodating, that it generally blends into
one of the most beautiful appendages of landscape.'[19]

The painter who sticks strictly to what he sees before him
'will rarely make a good picture'.[20] Nature is infinite, while
the artist could only ever be confined to a small part of it and
so he had to lay down rules. It was these rules that became
enshrined as the principles of picturesque beauty. He 'has no
right,' Gilpin set down, clarifying the parameters, 'to add a
magnificent castle – an impending rock – or a river, to adorn
his fore-ground. These are *new features*. But he may certainly
break an ill-formed hillock; and shovel the earth about him as
he pleases, without offence. He may pull up a piece of awkward
paling – he may throw down a cottage – he may even turn the
course of a road, or a river, a few yards on this side, or that.
These trivial alterations may greatly add to the beauty of his

composition; and yet they interfere not with the truth of the portrait.'[21]

Capturing the moment was not part of Gilpin's repertoire. He had a deep, inbuilt vision of 'rightness' and rather little curiosity about what lay behind the views that rolled past him and his party on their voyage down the river. He has no comment to make on the creeping industrialisation of the landscape they are passing through or on the squalor and poverty of the lives of those who lived there; the charcoal burners, for instance, who produced the fuel that the furnaces consumed. All he comments on, appreciatively, is the smoke 'which is frequently seen issuing from the sides of the hills; and spreading it's thin veil over a part of them, beautifully breaks their lines, and unites them with the sky.'[22] He is taken, though, by the story of a man who took his round, pitch-coated coracle from the New Weir (near Whitchurch) to Lundy Island in the Bristol Channel. When he came back – he could only have moved back up the river in the slack water between tides – 'the account of his expedition was received like a voyage round the world.'[23]

Gilpin, like most others who made the expedition down the Wye from Ross to Monmouth, had secured a covered boat, manned by three boatmen. (As he observed, they did not need such strength to carry them down the river. The real labour was the rowing back.) He was by no means the first to make this journey. More than thirty years earlier, the future Bishop of Durham, John Egerton, then Rector of Ross, had had a boat built to take his friends comfortably on trips down the Wye. Other boatmen were quick to see the commercial possibilities of such trips and soon there was a small fleet of tourist craft on the river, all rigged up with awnings against the weather and special tables where landscape tourists could make their sketches and catch up with their travel diaries.

Like tourist guides today, who at predetermined points unpen their charges from a bus to snap a particular view, the boatmen soon adopted a set itinerary, putting in front of their passengers all the things they had been told they must see. By 1794, twelve years after Gilpin published his *Observations*, the Monmouth Picnic Club set up a two-storey belvedere on the Kymin above the town. Members paid sixpence each to use the banqueting room and admire the views from the five, carefully positioned windows. There were, of course, instructions on how to look at each view in the properly picturesque manner.

It rained almost the entire time that Gilpin and his party were on the river. Nevertheless, at Monmouth, he was persuaded to send his coach away and continue the journey down to Chepstow with the object chiefly of seeing Tintern, the great Cistercian abbey founded by Walter de Clare, Lord of Chepstow, in 1131. Gilpin had high hopes of Tintern, already established as one of the most beautiful sights to be seen in the environs of the Wye. But he was disappointed. The abbey didn't sit in the landscape in the way he required. He felt let down by the fact that there was no opportunity to see the building as a distant object, which he had expected. The ruins themselves weren't correctly ruined – parts of it were beautiful, but the whole he deemed to be

ill-shaped. No ruins of the tower are left, which might give form, and contrast to the buttresses, and walls. Instead of this, a number of gabel-ends hurt the eye with their regularity; and disgust it by the vulgarity of their shape. A mallet judiciously used (but who durst use it?) might be of service in fracturing some of them; particularly those of the cross isles, which are not only disagreeable in themselves, but confound the perspective.[24]

Poor Gilpin, imprisoned in a straitjacket of his own making.

But if, as a landscape tourist, you'd had painting lessons from an even half-competent painting master, you'd know how to soften the irritatingly hard straight lines of the Tintern ruins with softening swags of ivy. You might even, in your mind's eye, be able to give it a more 'suitable' setting. John Byng, visiting in 1781,[25] couldn't understand why the Duke of Beaufort, who owned the place, didn't just sweep away the surrounding hovels so the abbey could stand 'nobly back'd by woods'. The proper way to enjoy Tintern, said the cynical Byng, was 'to bring wines, cold meat, with corn for the horses . . . Spread your table in the ruins; and possibly a Welsh harper may be procured from Chepstow.' A tourist attraction, the ruin had become an important source of income for local people. Byng himself 'enter'd the abbey accompanied by a boy who knew nothing, and by a very old man who had forgotten everything; but I kept him with me, as his venerable grey beard, and locks, added dignity to my thoughts; and I fancied him the hermit of the place.'

Yet for Samuel Palmer, incomparable Palmer, Tintern was altogether a vision of loveliness. 'Such an Abbey!' he wrote to the artist George Richmond: 'the lightest Gothic trellised with ivy & rising from a wilderness of orchards & set like a gem amongst the folding of woody hills.' His image, made in 1835 in pencil and bodycolour, shows the despised gable ends prominent against a flowing backdrop of wooded hills. By the following day, however, Palmer's rapture had lessened considerably. 'Poetic vapours have subsided,' his letter continued, 'and the sad realities of life blot the field of vision . . . I have not cash enough to carry me to London – O miserable poverty! How it wipes off the bloom from everything around me.'[26]

William Blake, *Sabrina's Silvery Flood* from *The Pastorals of Virgil* (1821)

CHAPTER 3

A Fitting Landscape

PALMER'S MYSTICAL, ECSTATIC response to landscape sets him in a different universe to Gilpin, with his rules and sidepieces. But why is it that some places call out to us, give us sustenance, and others don't? What anchored Constable to Suffolk, Wordsworth to the Lakes, Palmer to Shoreham and the Darenth valley? And when we leave our settled places to explore landscapes that are not our own, are we consciously looking for certain things? Or are we unconsciously imprinted, like Konrad Lorenz's goslings attaching to the first thing they see, with an idea of what a pleasing landscape should be? I was thinking about this as I paddled along the north Norfolk Coast Path one autumn, with the rain seeping through the shoulders of my waterproof. Because I was born among mountains, am I doomed for ever to be a misfit in the flat marshlands of the east? For there I was in an Area of Outstanding Natural Beauty, a Site of Special Scientific Interest, an UNESCO Biosphere Reserve, an EEC Special Protection Area, and the earth was not moving for me one millimetre.

I see a coastline in terms of cliffs and edges; it's what I was brought up on, during endless childhood summers in Pembrokeshire. Here in Norfolk, the land and the water twisted round each other like a nest of snakes. There were no edges. No cliffs. The sea was round a long corner from a harbour, or over the other side of sand dunes, or swallowed up in acres of salty reed beds. I wanted to be awed by north

Norfolk: the loneliness, the skies, the calls of geese flying low over the marshes. But the noise of the traffic on the coast road was always more insistent than any bird cries. And with its endless notice boards, its caravan sites, its car parks, its carefully laid boardwalks, it seemed a pretty tame wilderness to me. About as lonely as Southend-on-Sea.

'What brought *you* to these parts?' I asked a man in a pub, desperately searching for a good reason for being there. 'It's the only place in this country', he said, 'where you can see the sun both rise and set over the sea.' That was certainly a good reason to come, but I missed out on the sun. The rain continued inexorably the whole weekend. Tea shops had never looked more tempting; pub fires were never more difficult to leave. But I tried. I remember setting off from the Lifeboat Inn at Thornham to find the sea. A dead straight lane led down to the remains of a harbour, one of many that once existed along this coast, now beached as the sea drifts further and further away. Wells is now the only working harbour left, and that wouldn't be there without the dredger, pitted in an unequal struggle against the endlessly shifting sand.

Marshes lie to the east of the muddy Thornham creek. The coastal footpath skirts that area, so you have to go west, first along the top of a dyke which follows the edge of sunken fields, and then out into dunes. Beyond the dunes is a vast sweep of sand which turns the corner on the bump of Norfolk to face west across the Wash. When I was there it was low water, and the battered posts of an old groyne – evidence of an earlier attempt to check erosion – stood out blackly against the sand. 'That groyne', said a man fishing from the shore for dab, 'has not been seen in living memory until now.' It had appeared after a particularly bad storm, which also licked fifteen yards off the front of the dunes. A yard or so of sand had been scoured off the beach revealing not only the groyne but, out at the water's edge, shelves of dark peat, embedded with shells.

Until about 7000 BC, Norfolk was joined on to mainland Europe by a North Sea landscape of forest, swamp and brackish pools. The sea, rising in level, eventually drowned this land bridge, but here were its remains. You could make out the shape of roots and whole trees, lying where they had fallen, pickled now to a dark, crumbly softness. Impermanence makes an uneasy landscape in the wider sense, but in close-up, the beach was riveting. The currents were complex, explained the fisherman, who caught four dabs every day for his tea. When the fish came in on the tide, they crossed in front of him, parallel with the shore. The water then swirled round to the side and cut round the back of a higher bank of sand. On an incoming tide, you could suddenly find that your beach had turned into an island.

The sand was patterned with the marks of this swirling, capricious movement. Some areas of the beach were as smooth as veneer, others as frenetic as ruched curtains. In some places, the sand was mounded in gritty slopes, thick with shells: mussels, oysters, finely fluted piddocks and clams. The same richness of texture shows in the buildings of Norfolk too. At Holme-next-the-Sea (which isn't next at all) you see cottages built of stone the colour of raisin bread. Some are built of melting blocks of chalk. Most are made of combinations of brick and flint. There is very little stone in these parts and what there is (carstone) does not stretch far inland from this eastern edge. The flints, either knapped and used shiny edge out, or embedded whole, make intricately patterned frontages. Small fragments of brick are sometimes set like cherries in the lines of mortar between the flints. Small pebbles were used too, pressed in mortar in the same way, to make garden walls or to pattern gable ends.

In the pub, when I got back to it, people were still eating lunch, surrounded by the carefully stage-managed remnants of a civilisation now vanished: walls hung with reed cutters, rick knives, spokeshaves. Outside, the darkness that had been hovering all day finally collapsed on the flat marshes. I'd picked the pub from a guide. So, I guessed, had many other people there. There was not that sense of an interrupted programme that you get when you walk into a proper local that is not your own.

The following day, I started my coast walk at Burnham Deepdale, hovering in the church, hoping the rain might stop. Sinuous lions wind around the rim of the superb square Norman font there, a series of vignettes making a calendar of the seasons underneath. March shows a man goose-stepping with a spade. In November he is slaughtering a pig. There was more: medieval stained glass in the window of the tower, and fragments of rich cobalt blue gathered into a stunning little window behind the pulpit. Listening to the rain beating on the roof, it was tempting to draw out indefinitely the business of reading the tombstones on the walls.

But eventually I stepped out, because I still felt that somewhere along this coast there was going to be a moment when it suddenly grabbed the soul. I wanted it to. I was ripe for conversion. My road to Damascus lay first inland along a straight, straight lane (you can always see too far ahead of you in Norfolk), up a hill, a dizzy seventy feet high, on Barrow Common where, on a clear day, there might well have been a good view of the sea. The path over the common had the tired air of too many feet upon it, and the signs Private, No Entry, No Through Road to the Sea spoke of an area overburdened with tourists. Coming down off the Common, I padded through the barbed-wire footpaths of Brancaster and emerged by the mussel pits of the marsh side.

That was good. The place had purpose and also the pleasant litter of patched buildings that you get on the best sort of allotments. After that it was downhill all the way along the foreshore back to Burnham Deepdale. The narrow boardwalk made you feel as though you were toothpaste being squeezed out of a tube. The path led between piles of garden rubbish put out by the householders who live all along the shore. Even the sound of the curlews couldn't make up for the unremittingly lowering nature of this walk.

'Wells might be fun,' I thought to myself in rather a desperate way. It might be, but not on the wet Sunday afternoon I was there, when only amusement arcades leered out of the greyness. I pushed on east. Stiffkey had its back to the sea, which seemed sensible, and was shielded from it by a slight rise in the ground. It made all the difference, but the conversion I'd been hoping for never happened. Perhaps it was the wrong walk, taking me through a landscape that had been degraded, emasculated, absolutely worn out. It was certainly the wrong weather. But the real reason it failed to enchant, I fear, is because it was just too flat. As well as beauty, I need a certain majesty in a landscape, a sense of awe.

Northumberland, now Northumberland can give you that. Northumberland gives you long views; masses of trees, especially beech, often planted in avenues along minor roads; small stone towns with drapers and ironmongers still intact; and in the countryside, a pleasing sense of self-reliance. It's as though Newcastle and Gateshead have sucked in their breath and drawn everything urban down into one corner. Northumberland is left, empty of sprawl. Empty of many ways of making a living either, I couldn't help thinking, as I passed pasture after pasture too full of Roman-nosed Cheviot sheep. I've never thought of a sheep being an imperious creature, but these are. They are vast and rather stately, compared with the scraggy, thin-legged Welsh mountain sheep that I grew up with. The Cheviots hold their heads high, intent, like hammy screen stars, on offering their best profiles to passers-by.

The hedges are full of rowan trees, bent down in autumn with clusters of red berries. It's a tree I associate much more with the north of the country than the south. It puts up with poor soil. It grows on higher ground than most other trees. And it has the useful property of seeing off witches. English folklore is whimsical territory, but in among all that diaphanous stuff about elves and fairies, there are a few rock-solid themes: hawthorn is dangerous inside, but not out; four-leaved clovers bring luck; rowan will protect. At the Pitt Rivers anthropological museum, down the road from Keble College in Oxford, three knotted rowan twigs from Yorkshire are displayed in a case. Two of them came from the railings in front of a Dr Alexander's house at Castleton. The third was hooked over the gate by the porch of Castleton's church. They were there to protect against witchcraft, placed, so the museum caption says, 'by a horseman who turned his horse thrice before setting each loop'. Homes, crops, cattle, sheep – the rowan defended them all. If you didn't have a tree in the garden, you cut a branch and stuck it above the door of the house or stable. A rowan walking stick was a handy extra – the only way to pull a friend out of a witch's clutches.

Rowans sprout out of the most unlikely places on Hadrian's Wall. I walked the switchback section that goes past Crag Lough, where a great escarpment of rock suddenly rears up out of the moorland with this strange, dark, peaty catchment of water at its base. I wouldn't swim across it. Not for a thousand pounds. Some water is like that. Eerie. Noises like sheep bells came from the clinking gear of rock climbers, belayed out like stick insects from the vertical sandstone cliffs that rise from the lough.

The Great Whin Sill makes a natural escarpment right across Northumberland, all the way from Greenhead, on the Cumbrian border, to Bamburgh Castle on the coast, and the Romans made the most of it. I had not been to the wall before and supposed it would be made like a drystone wall, with random, gathered stone. Instead, here are regular, squared-off blocks, laid in neat parallel courses. It's craft of genius, twelve feet high when it was first made. By the time the Venerable Bede wrote about it in the eighth century, the stone had already been robbed for other building and the wall stood at eight feet. Now it is about five.

How tidy of the Romans to mark off their empire in this way, I thought. Clever too, since they chose to span the gap where England is at its narrowest. But a hellish place to be stationed, if you were one of the auxiliaries hauled over from mainland Europe and dumped, cold and wet, at this lonely outpost. Our landscape is full of ghosts, of hands that have twitched and pulled it into sheep runs and cattle folds, bridle-ways and burial mounds. It is one of its great strengths. With the wind howling round my hair, I thought of the last desperate message sent from England to the Romans, after they had abandoned us for ever. 'To Agitius, three times Consul, come the groans of the Britons . . . The barbarians drive us to the sea, the sea drives us to the barbarians; between the two means of death we are either killed or drowned.'[1] Groans. Gloom. High drama. Sublime landscape.

The problem with the sublime is that, like holding your breath, it is not a state you can sustain for long. But, like joy itself, it was easier to recognise the experience than describe it or its causes. For Joseph Addison, writing in the *Spectator* (Monday 23 June 1712), distance could be added to Burke's criteria of vastness, terror, awe, self-annihilation:

> a spacious horizon is an image of liberty, where the eye has room to range abroad, to expatiate at large on the immensity of its views, and to lose itself amidst the variety of objects that offer themselves to its observation. Such wide and undetermined prospects are as pleasing to the fancy, as the speculations of eternity or infinitude are to the understanding.[2]

Other essayists wandered in long elegant sentences through the concept of distance, to reach the unremarkable conclusion that 'Space, extended in length, makes not so strong an impression as height or depth.'[3] There was general agreement that, as the Scottish poet James Beattie put it,

> the most perfect models of sublimity are seen in the works of nature. Pyramids, palaces, fireworks, temples, artificial lakes and canals, ships of war, fortifications, hills levelled and caves hollowed by human industry, are mighty efforts, no doubt, and awaken in every beholder a pleasing admiration; but appear as nothing, when we compare them, in respect of magnificence, with mountains, volcanoes, rivers, cataracts, oceans, the expanse of heaven, clouds and storms, thunder and lightning, the sun, moon, and stars. So that, without the study of nature, a true taste in the sublime is absolutely unattainable.[4]

These eighteenth-century theories on the sublime (and the picturesque) shifted for ever the way that landscape was perceived. In 1685 the doughty traveller Celia Fiennes had been delighted to leave the chaos of the Lake District behind her (though she liked the waterfalls) and chose not to go on into Cumberland where 'I should have found more such and they tell me farr worse for height and stonynese.'[5] Cultivated landscapes, with their reassuring sense of order and promise of plenty, were far more congenial to her. Daniel Defoe, in his *Tour thro' the whole island of Great Britain* (1724–7) felt much the same, writing off the Lakes landscape as 'the wildest, most barren and frightful of any that I have passed over in England, or even in Wales itself'.[6] In the late seventeenth century, wild nature was still considered a threat to man's livelihood; the hills of the Lake District an irritating, not to say dangerous inconvenience to a civilised traveller.

But even after the great shift towards landscape had happened, much of the literature inspired by it, many of the paintings of dramatic sites such as Gordale Scar in Yorkshire and Snowdon's famous peak, were made by writers and artists passing through, on the move, gathering sketches, phrases, inspiration for work that would be finished off in the places, often cities, where they actually lived. Landscape for them was a sought-out experience. Yet there were important exceptions, where an artist or writer, born in a particular place, maintained a particular affinity with its landscape; where the landscape of a place was not a new experience but a familiar backdrop. Richard Wilson, born at Penegoes, Montgomeryshire, in 1713/14, used to say that, 'Everything the landscape painter could want, was to be found in North Wales.'[7] John Constable, after trying out some of the famous landscapes of the north, accepted how inexorably he was hefted to the Stour Valley in Suffolk, and returned to his conviction that 'I should paint my own places best.'[8]

John Constable, *A Summerland*, engraved by David Lucas for *Various Subjects of Landscape, Characteristic of English Scenery* (1831)

CHAPTER 4

'I Should Paint my own
Places Best'

PACING ROUND THE rooms of the Spring Gardens exhibition of watercolours in 1810, the correspondent of *Ackermann's Repository* noted the overwhelming proportion of landscapes in the show. His feelings, he wrote, were 'somewhat similar to those of an outside passenger on a mail-coach making a picturesque and picturizing journey to the North. Mountains and cataracts, rivers, lakes, and woods, deep romantic glens and sublime sweeps of country, engage his eye in endless and ever-varying succession.'[1] The revolution in taste that brought about this cascade of landscapes was in part a consequence of the war with France. Earlier in the eighteenth century, gentlemen of leisure embarked on a Grand Tour of France, Switzerland and Italy and reckoned their taste in Claudes. But the only practical way to get to the Classical landscapes of Claude and Poussin was by way of France. When that route became closed, new subjects had to be found. And national honour was perhaps involved. It was a patriotic thing to paint your own mountains, your own rocks and rivers, and to show that they could be made to look just as beautiful as anything a foreign country might have to offer. It was another way of fighting the French. Rich landowners raised monuments to the gallantry of Britain's navy in general and Nelson in particular (there's a beauty, put up in 1806, that looms up suddenly at the entrance to a cornfield on the Duncombe estate, North Yorkshire, dedicated 'To the memory of Lord Viscount Nelson and the unparalleled gallant achievements of the British Navy'), while the craggy landscape of Cumberland and Westmorland stood in for the Alps and Constable's calm landscapes of the Stour Valley replaced Claude's views of the Roman *campagna*. 'O England!' wrote Wordsworth,

> dearer far than life is dear,
> If I forget thy prowess, never more
> Be thy ungrateful son allowed to hear
> Thy green leaves rustle, or thy torrents roar![2]

John Constable (1776–1837) had the same good fortune as Wordsworth: to be born into a landscape that fed his soul. 'Painting is but another word for feeling,' he wrote to his friend John Fisher, Archdeacon at Salisbury Cathedral. 'I associate my "careless boyhood" to all that lies on the banks of the Stour. They made me a painter.'[3] He was fortunate, too, in being born into the family of a prosperous mill owner and corn merchant, Golding Constable, who if not exactly encouraging, at least did not thwart his second son's desire to become a painter. In 1806, a wealthy uncle paid for Constable to 'do' the Lakes, still considered part of a painter's education, a possible wellspring of inspiration, but it was not his sort of place. 'I have heard him say the solitude of mountains oppressed his spirits,' wrote C. R. Leslie. 'His nature was peculiarly social and could not feel satisfied with scenery, however grand in itself, that did not abound in human associations. He required villages, churches, farm-houses, and cottages.'[4]

But as well as loving the Stour Valley in East Anglia, Constable understood its significance as a working landscape.

Many of the landscape artists working at the same time were producing more conventional images of the picturesque, the beautiful or the sublime. If there are people in their mountainous scenes of North Wales or the Lake District, they often have their backs to the person looking at the painting. Frequently they will be gesturing towards the peak, the crag, the waterfall. This is what is important. The people in Constable's *Scene on a Navigable River (Flatford Mill)* are not there to direct the eye or to give scale. The young boy, barefoot on the back of the draught horse in the foreground, knows he has an important role. And by the confident ease of his position, looking back at the bargeman, his right hand splayed out on the horse's rump, we know it too. The bargeman, with his foot steadying the rope coiled on the foredeck, leans hard into the quant, pushing round the bow of the boat. That's exhausting work and Constable makes us feel it. But when the picture was exhibited at the Academy in 1817, it failed to find a buyer. Constable was fifty-three before he was elected a Royal Academician. Turner had been given the honour when he was only twenty-seven.

Part of the problem (as the grandees of the Royal Academy saw it) was Constable's technique, which produced landscapes of an unusually rough, scumbled texture, at a time when the accepted mode was smoother, more varnished. Solomon Hart recalled that,

Calling on Constable one day, I found him with a palette knife, on which was some white, mixed with a viscous vehicle, and with which he touched the surface of a beautiful picture he was painting. Upon expressing my surprise, he said, 'Oh! My dear Hart, I'm giving my picture the dewy freshness.' He maintained that the process imparted the dewy freshness of nature, and he contended that the apparent crudeness would readily subside, and that the chemical change which would ensue in a short time, would assume the truthful aspect of nature.[5]

The critic John Eagles was not convinced. Writing in *Blackwood's Magazine*, he said that Constable's oil painting, *The Valley Farm*, exhibited at the Royal Academy in 1835, looked as if it had been 'powdered over with the dredging box, or to have been under an accidental shower of white lead – which I find on enquiry is meant to represent the sparkling of dew. The sparkling of dew! . . . Such conceited imbecility is distressing, and being so large [the canvas measured 58in x 49¼in], it is but magnified folly.'[6]

The horizon of *Scene on a Navigable River,* as in so many of Constable's paintings, is set a little less than halfway up the frame. Skies, he wrote to John Fisher, 'must and always shall with me make an effectual part of the composition. It will be difficult to name a class of Landscape in which the sky is not the "*key note*", the "*standard of Scale*", and the chief "*Organ of sentiment*" . . . . The sky is the "*source of light*" in nature – and governs every thing.'

Constable understood that landscape had to be minutely studied. The execution of a painting was only a means to an end – the end being to reproduce the delight, the awe, the sustenance we get from the real thing. When we look at a good landscape painting, we ought to be able to feel the wind on our faces, see the clouds almost in movement, chasing each other through the sky. But each person will bring to the painting a different set of associations and memories. And each painting will represent a struggle on the part of the artist to fix a moment in a landscape that changes every second. Clouds group and reform; they drop over a line of moor; they lift; they are pierced by strange beams of light, which intensify the colours on which they shine. Rowan trees flame into being. The leaves of autumn ash trees blaze, momentarily, a shocking yellow as the spotlight moves over them.

The unusually specific titles of the twenty-two mezzotints David Lucas prepared for Constable's *Various Subjects of Landscape* (published in London in 1833) mark his determination to capture and still a particular moment in a particular place: *Spring. East Bergholt Common, Hail Squalls. – Noon*; *Stoke Church, By Neyland, Suffolk. – Rainbow at Noon*; *Head of a Lock on the Stour. Rolling Clouds*; *Barges on the Stour: Gleams of Light on the Meadows*; *A Water Mill, Dedham. – Burst of Light at Noon*; *Weymouth Bay, Dorset. – Tempestuous Evening*; *The Nore, Hadleigh Castle – Morning, after a Stormy Night*. His scenes, he wrote, 'are taken from real places, and are meant particularly to characterize the scenery of England; the effects of light and shadow being transcripts only of such as occurred at the time of being taken'.[7]

Constable had gathered together these landscapes 'to increase the interest for, and promote the study of, the Rural Scenery of England, with all its endearing associations, its amenities, and even in its most simple localities; abounding as it does in grandeur, and every description of Pastoral Beauty'. Its aim, he explained, was 'to direct attention to the source of one of its most efficient principles, the "CHIAR'OSCURO OF NATURE", to mark the influence of light and shadow upon Landscape . . . and to render permanent many of those splendid but evanescent Exhibitions, which are ever occurring in the changes of External Nature.'[8]

The time of day is particularly important, in terms of how the shadows fall on a particular scene. So is the season. In *Spring. East Bergholt Common, Hail Squalls. – Noon* he notes, 'the value of the vivid greens and yellows, so peculiar to this season'. Commenting on *Summer Morning. – The Vale of Dedham*, he writes:

> Nature is never seen, in this climate at least, to greater per-
> fection than at about nine o'clock in the mornings of July and
> August, when the sun has gained sufficient strength to give
> splendour to the landscape . . . It may be well to mention
> the different appearances which characterize the Morning
> and Evening effects. The dews and moisture which the earth
> has imbibed during the night cause a greater depth and cool-
> ness in the shadows of the Morning; also, from the same
> cause, the lights are at that time more silvery and sparkling;
> the lights and shadows of Evening are of a more saffron or
> ruddy hue, vegetation being parched during the day from
> the drought and heat.[9]

The mezzotints were taken from various pictures that Constable had exhibited at the Royal Academy, and of the twenty-two, fifteen were of scenes in Suffolk. His view of Weymouth Bay in Dorset was taken while on honeymoon there in the autumn of 1816. Later sojourns in Hampstead and Brighton were prompted by his wife's ill health. He did not like Brighton, complaining to Fisher in August 1824 that the place was nothing but 'the receptacle of the fashion and off-scouring of London. The magnificence of the sea and its (to use your own beautifull expression) everlasting voice, is drowned in the din & lost in the tumult of stage coaches – gigs – "flys" etc. – and the beach is only Piccadilly . . . by the sea side . . . In short there is nothing here for a painter but the breakers – & sky.' He made the most of the breakers, includ-ing *A Sea Beach, Brighton, Heavy Surf. –Windy Noon* as one of the subjects of his collection of mezzotints. 'The magnitude of a coming wave when viewed beneath the shelter of a Groyne . . . is most imposing,' he wrote. He remarked, too, on the 'sentiment of melancholy always attendant on the ocean'.

Constable was out of step with his time, but he never wavered from his belief that, at East Bergholt, and in the Vale of Dedham, he had an idyll that could not be bettered. Writing to accompany a mezzotint of East Bergholt, he declared,

> The beauty of the surrounding scenery, the gentle declivi-ties, the luxurious meadow flats sprinkled with flocks and herds, and well cultivated uplands, the woods and rivers, with farms and picturesque cottages, all impart to this par-ticular spot an amenity and elegance hardly anywhere else to be found; and which has always caused it to be admired by all persons of taste, who have been lovers of Painting, and who can feel a pleasure in its pursuit when united with the contemplation of Nature.
>
> Perhaps the Author, in his over-weaning affection for these scenes may estimate them too highly, and may have dwelt too exclusively upon them; but interwoven as they are with his thoughts, it would have been difficult to have avoided doing so; besides, every recollection associated with the Vale of Dedham must always be dear to him, and he delights to retrace those scenes, 'where once his careless childhood strayed'.[10]

Towards the end of his life, Constable gave a series of lectures on landscape, first (17 June 1833) to the members of the Literary and Scientific Society of Hampstead, then to the Worcestershire Institution for Promoting Literature. His talk, reported the correspondent of the *Worcester Herald* of 10 October 1835, gave 'very beautiful and feeling illustrations of the parentage and birth of the art, and . . . called forth repeated remarks of satisfaction and delight'. Encouraged by the success he had had with these audiences, he expanded his initial talk into a series of lectures which he gave at the Royal Institution in London, starting on 26 May 1836 and continuing on the next four Thursdays until 16 June. Dürer was his first hero, followed, in the second lecture, by Claude, whose paintings he described as 'the calm sunshine of the heart'. In Lecture Three he turned to the Dutch and Flemish Schools, Rubens in particular, who like Constable delighted in 'dewy light and freshness'. In his final talk, Constable considered the revival of landscape painting in the hands of John Robert Cozens and Thomas Girtin, Thomas Gainsborough ('soothing, tender, and affecting') and above all, Richard Wilson (1713/14–1782). 'To Wilson', he said,

> may justly be given the praise of opening the way to the genuine principles of Landscape in England; he appeared at a time when this art, not only here, but on the Continent, was altogether in the hands of the mannerists . . . He looked at nature entirely for himself, and remaining free from any tincture of the styles that prevailed among the living artists, both abroad and at home, he was almost wholly excluded from any share of the patronage which was liberally bestowed on his contemporaries.'[11]

Though they shared the fate of feeling – and being – undervalued in their lifetimes, the trajectory of the two men could not have been more different. Constable, who married a rich wife, never had to worry about the financial implications of his

paintings failing to sell. Wilson deliberately abandoned a lucrative career as a portrait painter in Italy to reinvent himself as a
painter of landscapes, and died in obscure poverty. Constable,
rooted in the flat lands of East Anglia, has affinities (if
anywhere) with the Dutch landscape tradition. Wilson, who
grew up in North Wales with Cader Idris broodily massive
in front of his father's rectory, and Plynlimmon (itself
2,467 ft high) at the back, nevertheless brought to his British
landscapes something of his time in Italy.

Some saw this as a fault. Not Constable. After a visit to
Sir John Leicester's picture gallery in 1823 he told Fisher
that he recollected 'nothing so much as a solemn – bright –
warm – fresh landscape by Wilson, which still swims in
my brain like a delicious dream. Poor Wilson. Think of his
magnificence, think of his fate!' The painting was of Tabley
House in Cheshire, made by Wilson around 1764, when he
was still perhaps hoping that by sliding from portraits of
people to portraits of houses, he might, by sleight of hand
almost, lead his patrons to an appreciation of landscape
per se. But he was working at a time when the theorists and
taste makers still set history painting at the top of a hier-
archy of subjects 'suitable', in intellectual terms, for great
paintings. Landscape, along with still lives and pictures of
animals, sat at the bottom. History painting, with its allu-
sions to classical themes, could claim intellectual kinship
with philosophy and literature. Landscapes, even ones
washed over with a Roman light, as Wilson's often were,
could not. At Bowood, in the late 1760s, Lord Shelburne
was ahead of his time in commissioning paintings from
Wilson, Thomas Gainsborough and George Barrett, with
the intention of laying 'the foundation of a school of British
landscape'. It didn't happen then and only death relieved

Wilson, who came to be considered the 'father' of landscape painting in Britain, from 'the neglect of a tasteless
public' that Fuseli had noted.[12]

Perhaps his most appreciative customers were, as Oliver
Fairclough suggests, 'Welsh landowners with antiquar-
ian interests'.[13] For William Vaughan of Cors y Gedol, a
prominent figure in the Celtic Revival of the later eighteenth century, he painted his breath-held view of *Snowdon
from Llyn Nantlle* (1765–6), the great mountain rearing up
behind the mirror surface of the lake in the foreground. The
young Sir Watkin Williams-Wynn, a generous patron of the
arts, commissioned two big landscapes, including *View near
Wynnstay* (1770–71), his family seat; Wilson's painting shows
not the house but a long view west along the River Dee to
Dinas Bran at Llangollen.

Wilson's most famous painting *Llyn-y-Cau, Cader Idris*
(1765–7) was of a landscape that was only seven miles from
his first home at Penegoes. He is standing, as it were, high
on the slopes of Mynydd Moel looking across the still, dark
waters of the volcanic lake to the almost sheer rocky ridge
of Craig Cau behind. Diminutive figures in the foreground
suggest the immense scale of the view. One person looks out
through a telescope to Cardigan Bay on the horizon. A second
sits on the grass sketching, while a third (the guide?) holds
a grey pony. The most famous guide in the area was Robin
Edwards, 'CONDUCTOR TO, and over the most tremendous mountain CADER IDRIS . . . GUIDE GENERAL and
MAGNIFICENT EXPOUNDER of all the natural and artificial
curiosities of North Wales', who always claimed the honour of
having been the first person to take the painter to the summit
of Cader Idris.

No one before Richard Wilson had ever painted this view, which subsequently became so famous that Llyn Cau became more popularly known as Wilson's Pool. When, a year before his death, he left London, a pauper, to be taken in by his cousin, Catherine Jones at Colmendy Hall near Mold, this painting was still in his possession.

J. M. W. Turner, *Ben Arthur, Scotland*, engraved by Thomas Lupton, from
Etchings and Engravings for the 'Liber Studiorum' (1819)

CHAPTER 5

The Highlands

FOR AN ARTIST or landscape tourist intent on collecting all the trump cards, a journey to Scotland had, somehow, to be arranged, despite the difficulties. In a practical sense, it was a far more complex undertaking than going to North Wales or the Lakes. For most tourists, it was much further away from their home territory, the country was far larger, longer distances had to be covered. But it also presented intellectual problems. In its magnificent wildness, its vastness, its emptiness, its wild, savage, uncageable grandeur, it was ill-suited to the prescriptive nature of picturesque principles. Scotland, in a way, was eventually responsible for shattering all those rules so carefully created and imposed by William Gilpin in his journey down the more tractable Wye. Travellers, such as Dorothy Wordsworth and her brother William, who were there in 1803, were already beginning to tire of being told what to look at and how to see it. At Blair Castle, one of the obligatory stopping places on the journey north, 'We submitted ourselves to the gardener,' the poet's sister wrote in her journal, 'who dragged us from place to place, calling attention to, it might be, half-a-dozen (I cannot say how many) dripping streams.'[1]

Gilpin, touring the country in 1776, tried to tug the place into shape, but though there were plenty enough rough tracks, grassy knolls and jagged rocks for his foregrounds, he complained that 'the Scotch distance rarely exhibits any diversity of objects'.[2] But Thomas Gray, a pioneering traveller in the

Highlands as he had been in the Lakes, found the Highlands 'extatic' and said that they 'ought to be visited in pilgrimage once a year'.[3] I was ridiculously slow in taking his advice.

I first fought my way into this territory by the high road that goes from Otterburn through Jedburgh. On a good day this route, swooping switchback over the moors, gives long views to the east over the Lammermuir Hills, well advertised in brown road signs and small fan-shapes on the road map. These prospects are mostly of one particular kind: as the word suggests, the views chosen for us by the tourist authorities and map makers are mostly taken from a high point which looks out over a distant and very wide spread of land beyond. It's an expression of power, perhaps, but the things we look at from these high places do not always give us the heightened emotions that, if we are lucky (and receptive), landscape is capable of delivering. Often, there's just too much land spread out there in front and it's all too far away. We are too detached from it.

That first time, heading to the Highlands by way of road signs that simply say The North, wild winds were blowing, and the rain lashed so hard against the windscreen I thought it would come through. Clouds sat heavy and low over whatever landscape there was out there. Even the car's headlights could not penetrate the gloom. But it's right to have to fight your way into such glory. On the far side of the Firth of Forth, the sun at last shone on the distant hills ahead. Though I was often looking at these patches of brightness through sudden veils of rain, they lay there like promises. And then I was in them, chasing along with the sunshine by Loch Lochy and Loch Loyne, past the dramatic silhouette of Eilean Donan Castle on the shores of Loch Duich, until I came to the most beautiful loch of them all, Loch Carron. Here the road shrunk to the kind of size I feel comfortable with. It would have been good at this stage to have abandoned the car altogether and continued by horse. But I didn't know that until I got there. Perhaps another time: an enigmatic meeting at Stromeferry (no ferry), the car whisked into limbo, a sturdy packhorse with panniers for my notebooks waiting to take me up into the mountains, which is where I want to be. Always.

The road squeezed along the side of Loch Carron, parallel with an equally small single-track railway (trains three times a day from Inverness to Kyle of Lochalsh, the stopping-off point for Skye). Sometimes you have views over the loch to the village of Lochcarron – single-storey stone houses spread out along the far shore of the loch. Sometimes, at a bend, you face the other way and confront instead the great flanks of mountains that lead eventually up to Loch Torridon, further north.

Of all the places in our shrinking island that can still deliver that sense of the sublime that Burke wrote about, the most potent, for me, is Wester Ross. Looking west into the sunset from the neat cottages on the shores of Loch Carron, the loch is a shining sheet. Very faint, very hazy on the horizon are the points of the Cuillins on Skye. Occasionally a low shaft of sunlight catches a wet rock face on the side of a hill and that shines too, until the beam moves on to highlight another unexpected feature of the landscape. In early spring, the colours on the hill are more dun, more fused together than they are in autumn. With the big trees in the gulleys bare of leaf, the hanging fringes of lichen on their branches, a strange sulphurous pale grey-green, take on a fluorescent, almost phosphorescent quality and shine out against the purplish-bronze wash of the birch twigs. In late March, that first time, there was still snow on the tops of the hills, losing itself in the bracken as it drifted lower down the slope.

After that first visit, not a year passed without my spending time in the Highlands. In summer, on the peaty moorland above the loch, sheets of wild orchids grow in the kind of damp, acid soil that does not encourage the lush growth of grass and weeds. Around the orchids is a particular kind of moss that grows in similar situations on the Black Mountains and Brecon Beacons, the Welsh border country where I grew up. It's the kind of moss that I associate with sundew. In Wales the two plants often grew together, the sundew's spoon-shaped, succulent, ground-hugging leaves glistening with a red tinge in the more subdued, matt surround of the moss. As a child, I kept a sundew as a pet, on a saucer on the kitchen windowsill. Ghoulishly I fed it insects that I trapped against the window panes. And here it was in Scotland too, in the same moss, but with the glorious addition of the orchids. No wonder it felt like home.

In the Highlands, each storm re-makes the landscape. Rain here is not always dispiriting, but can be a wild, liberating catalyst. Hills that have lain quietly in their tweedy coverings of buff and fox-brown, grey boulders and deep coloured moss, burst, with rain, into wild, noisy thunder. Water pours down gulleys that you barely noticed before. Dark creases in the hills, that you scarcely read in the wider landscape, suddenly become narrow, forceful falls, white ropes let down over the sides of the distant hills with astonishing suddenness.

Many of the hills here are slantingly cut with seams of rock among the small goldening birches and the bracken. Water tips from the edges of many of these seams to make its endlessly different ways down to the valleys. I'm thinking of one such seam where the water at first falls clasping the rock tight. But at a cliff face it splinters, one thread fracturing into a veil all over the wetly dark face. From there it disappears for a while into a deep gully worn in the rock, but then surges out again in a thick, white fall. Eventually this splinters into a delta of rivulets. Each storm reinvents the details of the physiognomy of the fall. It brings the hill alive: the noise, the movement, the intricate variation of each fall, within its own basic map. Just once, on a day in late March, when the hills were thunder-ing with snowmelt water, I saw at the bottom of a fall I often pass, a strange veil of light, not a rainbow but a shimmering miasma of rainbow colours, indistinct greenish yellow, blue, indigo, hovering over the rocks on which the water finishes its descent. I watched it until imperceptibly it faded away. I have never seen it since.

The because-it's-there factor that is said to drive mountaineers up ever more impossible peaks has no relevance in the search for good waterfalls. Quite often, they are *not* there. All depends on the weather, not necessarily at the point where the waterfall is, but way off in the hills beyond, where if conditions are propitious, it gradually gathers its power and substance. Waterfalls can't be captured in photographs, which increases their magic. Even the fastest blink of a shutter immobilises the falling water and makes it look like amateur ectoplasm. Video cameras catch some of the movement, but give little impression of height or depth of field. You have to be there. As you slowly approach a waterfall, its voice gradually fills your brain. Not all of them shout and thunder. Instead, they play variations on a theme that is constantly changing its pitch. Has anyone ever tried to notate its song?

On a whim, once, on my way to Wester Ross, I veered west from Fort William to poke my nose into the Kingairloch peninsula. The road I followed had a very pleasing, tentative, impermanent quality, the tarmac laid in a provisional way on ground which bucked and heaved under it like a lion covered with a blanket. At one point, it cantilevers out over the edge of Loch Linnhe, then plunges back inland to a place where the map showed a whole series of becks rising on Creach Bheinn (2,799 ft). It was obvious, from the contour lines on the map that they would be getting themselves very quickly from the high ground down to sea level. It's the kind of topography that often results in good waterfalls.

Creach Bheinn produced the goods that day. As I nosed at fifteen miles per hour through the inflexible rain, each turn in the track revealed a new cascade, torrenting down the steep cliff of the hill. The weather was too wild for me to get to them. In good weather, they wouldn't exist. So I watched them through my field glasses, lurching from delirium to rapture along that fortunately deserted road. It's the most exhausting thirteen miles I've ever travelled in a car.

Unexpected waterfalls such as these nearly always give more pleasure than the great set pieces. The Falls of Measach at Braemore in Ross-shire were certainly a disappointment: too close to a noisy main road and a burger van that filled the deep Corrieshalloch Gorge with the smell of stale fat. It could have been good. The river there falls 150 ft into a narrow box canyon which runs for a mile down the valley. John Fowler, who was one of the designers of the Forth Railway Bridge, built a handsome suspension bridge over the gorge, so you get an unusually good vantage point to look down the chasm. But of charisma, it has none.

The best waterfall on that particular trip was not the biggest or the loudest. But in many ways it was the most complex – a confluence of waterfalls – and we caught it when the late afternoon light was throwing long shadows over the glen and buzzards were wheeling overhead in the eddies of Slioch's peak. Walking in from Incheril, we followed the left-hand bank of the beck, called Abhainn an Fuirneis, from its end on the shore of Loch Maree to its beginning at Lochan Fada, high in the hills above.

The stream itself is remarkable, shooting from pool to pool by way of endless cascades and falls. Dwarfed Scots pine, natural bonsai, grow from improbably small cracks in the rock. Rowans hang over the banks. That stream on its own would be enough for any waterfall-fancier, but about halfway up it is joined by two much smaller streams coming down either side of the valley. On the right, the tributary drops in the fashion of Angel Falls – a single thin rope of water, always contained, never spreading. On the left, a fall appears over a precipice, thrown by the vagaries of the rock to make a wide, rippling blanket of water, foaming against the darkly glistening background. White noise. Black peaks. Unavoidably purple prose.

Benjamin Malkin wrote of a waterfall he'd seen that 'the luminous appearance of the foaming element . . . glittering as if with gems . . . could scarcely be represented on paper.'[4] But some painters tried: Jacob More, who started his career painting scenery for the New Theatre in Edinburgh, made in the 1770s a memorable trio of paintings, *Falls of Clyde*, showing the three great waterfalls of Bonnington Linn, Corra Linn and Stonebyres Linn. The falls, having already attracted the 'correct' literary connotations (in 1730 Corra Linn had starred in James Thomson's influential poem, *The Seasons*) became one of the first destinations in Scotland for the landscape tourist. Few of them showed as much interest in the New Lanark cotton mills, an industrial wonder of the age, situated only a few hundred yards downstream.

Corra Linn, heard before it was seen, produced an authentic experience of the Sublime. 'You are struck at once with the aweful scene which suddenly bursts upon your astonished sight . . . this great body of water, rushing with horrid fury, seems to threaten destruction to the solid rocks that enrage it by their resistance. It boils up from the caverns which itself has formed, as if it were vomited out of the lower regions. The horrid and incessant din with which this is accompanied, unnerves and overcomes the heart.'[5]

Paul Sandby had painted Bonnington Linn in about 1750, while he was still working as a draughtsman for the Military Survey of Scotland (1746–51). Turner went to the falls of the Clyde too, but Turner went everywhere. Before he was even twenty-six, he'd explored Derbyshire, the Midlands, East Anglia, the Isle of Wight, Yorkshire, Northumberland, County Durham, the Lakes, the Tweed, North and South Wales, Wiltshire as well as Scotland. He included *The Fall of the Clyde* as one of the subjects in his *Liber Studiorum,* a series of prints issued from 1807 onwards in which he intended, as the prospectus announced, 'to attempt a classification of the various styles of landscape, viz, the historic, mountainous, pastoral, marine, and architectural'.[6] The Falls print was classified as EP. Did that mean Elevated Pastoral, Edifying Pastoral, Epic Pastoral, Elegant Pastoral, Ecstatic Pastoral? Turner did not explain. But the noise, the force, the energy, the splintering mass of a waterfall, remaking itself in uncountable different modes, how could this possibly be captured? Only Turner could do it, not in the print of 1809, but in his oil painting of the falls, made c.1840,[7] form transmuted into force, line shattered into a swirling compound of air and water, sight and sound. Yes. Turner could do it.

By the time the nineteenth century was well under way, Romance, in the guise of Landseer and Walter Scott, had taken over the Highlands. But I can't see it as a Romantic landscape. There are too many ghosts in it for that. Not just the big ones – the massacre at Glencoe, the clearings – but smaller ones, just as potent in their way, that rise unexpectedly in your path. Like the marker, set by the side of the narrow road that runs along the north shore of Loch Torridon: 'This stone was erected in 1912 by Ann, widow of Duncan Darrock of Gourock and Torridon, in memory of the devotion and affection shown by one hundred men on the estate of Torridon, who at their own request carried his body from the house here on its way to interment in the family burying place at Gourock.' Then there's the weather. All landscape is mediated by weather but in the Highlands it seems particularly so. One day in mid-October I walked the lonely six-mile track through heather and whin from the bothy at Bendronaig to the cottage I was staying in at Attadale. There had been a hard frost the previous night and the yellow leaves of birches floated aimlessly from the trees. It was an absolutely still day when I started, clear sky, bright sunshine. Pointed arrowheads of trees rose from the deep gulleys either side of the track, the rowans flaring out brilliant red against the grey rock, the flat faces of the biggest boulders smeared like an artist's palette with encrusted lichens in tawny brown, orange, silver, pewter. At this season of the year, the moor grass is gingery, the dominant colour of the hills. Only where it is doing unusually well does it develop seed heads and produce patches of creamy-beige. The lochans that day were so still they appeared as voids, shocking black holes in the landscape. The track follows a stream, now wide and shallow, now pushed into a gulley and falling hard into a pool below, worn out by the endless wash of water. It was lovely. Then suddenly a harsh, strong, easterly wind got up. The sky began to press down on the land. The wind howled down the pass, bending the dead grasses, pulling from the pine trees the moaning that is one of the loneliest sounds on earth. I started to sing, always a bad sign.

The eighteenth-century scholar James Beattie described Scotland as 'in general a melancholy country' but 'in general' I have not found it so. Melancholy has been far outweighed by delight: watching cloud, drifting in shape-changing forms across the intricate tweed of the hills, or the bizarre pools of light that the sun suddenly throws on to a landscape, as tightly focused as a theatrical spotlight. For the sublime, you need go no further than the Applecross Peninsula and look west over five planes of alternating darkness and light towards Skye: foreground – island – water – island – mountain peaks. The Pool of Crowlin – Raasay – The Sound of Raasay – Skye – the Cuillinns. Looking into the sun (the best time) with the light coming in from the front-left, all colour goes from the landscape. We see the land as a series of silhouettes, cut-out shapes, the nearer ones darker, the far ones (the jaggiest) reading opaquely in only two dimensions. Land rising opaquely from the sea, the immense, glittering spread of the sea.

John Constable, *Yarmouth, Norfolk*, engraved by David Lucas, from
English Landscape Scenery (1855)

CHAPTER 6

Making the Journey

THE SEA WAS a long way from my childhood and there was an element almost of pilgrimage in the journeys we made to it each year. For twelve years it was always the same place, always the same way of reaching it: a series of slow, blunt-nosed buses that smelt of oil and damp plush. The journey took a whole day. The first leg took us from Abergavenny to Brecon, the second (the longest) from Brecon to Carmarthen, where there was a tricky cross-town manoeuvre with luggage to catch the third bus, to Haverfordwest.

During the final haul to our destination at Little Haven, through stone-banked lanes of scabious and yellow toadflax, there was a particular corner where you got your first glimpse of the sea, glinting at the end of a dip between two fields. Each year, at this point, I felt my head was going to shoot off the top of my body with excitement. I couldn't shout, or jump up and down. I just sat there, locked on to the view of the sea, with my head about to explode.

We spent the whole of the summer holidays in Little Haven, our days marked out by the times and the state of the tides. Were they springs or neaps? Could we climb round to our favourite, most inaccessible beach before lunch, or after? My mother and father didn't like sitting on beaches and walked clifftops instead, through heather, sea campion and mounds of papery thrift. But they expected my brother and me not to be idiots. So we weren't. During the day, we climbed from inlet to inlet, bay to bay, always on dropping tides, rather than rising ones. Sometimes we had to wait on a rocky peninsula for the tide to fall a little. On one, there was a rock pool coated with something the colour of coral. From a crevice on the side, a small silvery seaweed floated out like Ophelia's hair. I offered my finger to the tentacles of a sea anemone, and it sucked at it, before pulling back into its rust-coloured bag.

Each of these pools offered a different landscape, each made from a strange alliance of calm and chaos. We see the calm, but we can only imagine the chaos, as the tide crashes in on the pools, swirling, scouring, tugging at the seaweeds. And then retreating, leaving part of itself behind, connecting each of these small microcosms to its neighbour.

Honour demanded that, in our climbing, we shouldn't make things too easy for ourselves. Timing was everything. As a wave pulled out from a gulley, you jumped on to a rock that was only temporarily above water. As the sea gathered itself to knock you off, you jumped again, over the divide, landing, you hoped, on a ledge that wasn't too slippery with seaweed. The scariest thing we ever did was to scramble, climb and swim our way round from Little Haven to the Goultrop Roads. I never saw that name written down – maps then existed in our minds, not on paper. So I thought it was called Gold Drop: treasure, mystery and the possibility of locating the leather chest that must exist in the mind of anyone who has ever read Robert Louis Stevenson.

It was a weird place, with scrub oak and tattered syca-more dripping almost vertically from the cliff top to the sea.

It was about the only place on this coast sheltered from the south-westerlies and once there had been a lifeboat station here, a sailing lifeboat, with oars for twelve. It closed in the 1920s because there were never enough people to call on for a crew. Then a massive cliff fall tore away the fragile, vertiginous track leading down to the shoreline and Goultrop was sealed off – inaccessible except by sea.

Because it faced north, it was a dark place, and because it was sheltered from the prevailing wind, the sea there was uncannily still. The land dropped steep into the sea, which rose and fell to a barnacle line on the rocks, as though being sucked and expelled by some great lung on the seabed, which here was too deep to see. There was no beach, seemingly no bottom, and the water swirled thickly and slowly with brown weed – bladderwrack, saw wrack and the long clammy ribbons of oarweed. We dared each other to swim across Goultrop through the seaweed, not a dangerous thing to do, but terrifying if you are cursed with a fertile imagination. The dark woods watched. The dark water waited. The dark weed wrapped itself round us as we pushed through to the far side of the Roads. We did it. But we never did it again.

Now I can jump into the car, slam the doors on the luggage and be in Little Haven in a quarter of the time. If you are travelling with three small children and a dog, there are undeniable advantages in this. I do not miss staggering through Carmarthen with a suitcase about to pop its locks, nor worrying about the bus connection. We always made it, but the worry never went away. The car, though, is undeniably banal. The ease of it reduces the importance of the journey. I miss the ritual of the series of lumbering buses, the sense of pilgrimage to that miracle of the sea beyond the fields.

Speed diminishes the gifts that a journey can give you, the gift, for instance, of moving through a landscape slowly enough to be able to watch it, take in its characteristics, observe the land's relationship to the sky, the patterning made by boundaries, whether of hedge or stone, the way that trees, banks in the lanes signal changes in the underpinning of the landscape: limestone turning to chalk, clay to sandy loam. Travelling fast, especially on aeroplanes, there is not enough time to clear away the mental baggage you have brought with you from the ordinary and make a space in your mind for the extraordinary.

Aeroplanes came into my life immediately after the Pembrokeshire summers, in the period when all I wanted from a holiday was a good suntan. The means was not as important as the end. You just wanted to get to the hot spot as quickly as possible: Spain, Portugal, the Greek Islands, wherever. But when you are flying, detached from the landscaped world, wrapped in an ether of cloud, you have no sense of progressing towards a goal. There is only the start and finish of the journey: in between is a void. To appreciate a landscape as intricate as Britain's, we need to reinvent the sense of anticipation, slow down our approach so that the destination – beach, river, moor or mountain, the object of our dreams – advances imperceptibly, a place glimmering on the horizon that gradually grows to fill the whole of our minds.

Boats do it beautifully. It was what made Tresco in the Scilly Isles so special before it got a helicopter landing-pad. The helicopter (defunct now) used to go only as far as the biggest island, St Mary's. There, you made your way down to the quay where one of the Bryher boatmen would be waiting in an open boat to take you over the last stretch of water to Tresco's silvery landing stage. Pure masochism, some might

think. I think not. The point of an island is the water round it.
Arriving by sea, you are more aware of the influences that have
shaped this particular landscape, accepting, welcoming even,
its limitations.

But it depends on whether or not you think the journey
an important part of the arrival. In the age of sunbathing, I
did not. Nor would skiers, who just want to get to the snow
as quickly as possible. Now I see things differently. I want to
slow down the whole process, stay in touch with the business
of moving over the landscape. Cities can take care of themselves, but the smaller the destination, the more carefully you
need to match your arrival to it. You need to be careful, too,
when you are making a journey to a place that holds special
significance for you. It is too easy to wipe out that significance, to belittle the place by sweeping down on it with too
little ceremony.

I always salute Stonehenge when I pass it. Yet I feel bad,
storming home down the A303 with Eric Clapton pounding
away on the car's tape deck and a half-eaten Mars bar in my
hand. It seems disrespectful to flash by like this. Suddenly
there they are ahead, the stones, as you crest the brow of
the hill, and equally suddenly, gone. They do not have a
chance to speak of their consequence, their gravity, their
implications, their place in this complex ritual landscape
of our ancestors. Those of us who can, should have to walk
a considerable distance to find Stonehenge, to take it in as
it rises naked from the plain, to watch the rectangles of
sky between the monoliths change as we approach. If it is
raining, so much the better. No effort we make can rival
the effort made by its builders. We demean that by glancing
at it as we pass by at sixty miles per hour. The poor stones
are un-powered also by the fence that now surrounds them,

necessary though that may be. They are like performing elephants in a circus ring, trapped, caged. But sometimes, at half past five on a June morning, say, with a red sun suspended on the horizon, Stonehenge still breathes power. In that light, the barrier does not intrude; the stones, throwing long ghost shadows, regain their strength. We see them momentarily as William Turner of Oxford saw them, in the first half of the nineteenth century, standing in a landscape empty of anything but themselves. In the mid-ground of his watercolour, the land dips down into a smooth hollow with the enigmatic stones standing in silhouette on the horizon beyond.

A choice about how we travel is a luxury, of course, that the early seekers after landscape did not have. The Suffolk agriculturist, Arthur Young, travelling in North Wales in the 1770s, said the roads through the Welsh mountains were 'mere rocky lanes, full of hugeous stones as big as one's horse'.[1] Thomas Rowlandson made fun of the difficulties: too much rain, too much paraphernalia, unsatisfactory transport. His cartoon *An Artist Travelling in Wales* (a sly dig at William Gilpin) shows the lanky figure balanced on a pony three times too small, his feet in the stirrups almost dragging along the ground. In one hand he holds an umbrella, under his other arm is an unwieldy collapsible easel and strapped to his back are a couple of large canvases. The pony slithers down a steep slope, hung round like a market stall with bottles and baskets, palette and paints.

The advantage of travelling slowly was that it gave time to look. The painter Cornelius Varley, a great admirer of Richard Wilson's work, was particularly drawn to the landscapes in which Wilson had grown up, and travelled in North Wales in 1802, 1803 and 1805. Raised by his uncle, a maker of scientific instruments, Varley looked at landscapes with a scientist's as well as an artist's eye (in 1811 he patented a 'Graphic Telescope' which projected an image on to a flat surface where it could be more easily drawn or traced). On his 1805 journey he was alone. 'This apparent solitude', he wrote, 'mid clouds & mountains left me more at large "To hold converse with Nature's charms & view her stores untold."' Sitting on the north side of the Vale of Llanllyfni, south of Caernarfon, he watched a few small clouds floating over the southern range of the mountains with extraordinary attention:

These were moving eastwards and following each other correctly over the same summits, & the foremost led the way & passed direct over the Peak of Snowdon & then it assumed a pecululiar definite and stratified form, showing some decided action between the two, though they did not touch. The second and third followed exactly the same path and paid the same peculular respect as they passed Snowdon Peak. Some whilst passing over a vale left an end as lingering towards a hinder peak & sent out one towards a lateral peak whilst a foremost portion stretched out faster towards Snowdon. These hinder parts were gathered in when fairly over Snowdon, but when clearly past Snowdon they resumed their shapeless form, but while intending to watch the last over Snowdon I found there were quite as many others following, their number still increasing, & they were larger. I watched the hindermost one, it had little ragged portions of no account following, but they were swelling into clouds & passed on, & their minute rags were swelling after them at a greater rate toward the west than the wind could carry them east. They now obscured the outline of the southern range. Then rain began at the east and very slowly extended westward till the whole range was under rain. By this time the line of clouds had grown some miles over the sea, thus meeting the wind that fed them, the distant horizon being still visible under them, but the rain extended gradually to the sea and verry progressively obscured the distant horizon.

I had yet fine weather over head, but the clouds kept increasing in size till the whole sky was overcast & a cheerless rainy afternoon ensued – Here I believe I saw and understood the gradual progress from a cloudless morning to universal rain, here was a silent invisible flow of electricity to the mountains.[2]

The product of this intense, damp day in the mountains is distilled in his landscape *Snowdon from Llanllyfni* in the Birmingham Museum and Art Gallery.

Journeys, of course, had to be made mostly in late spring and summer, when an artist could build up a stock of drawings and watercolours to work up during the winter into finished paintings which he hoped might suit the market. Varley was an early member of The Society for the Study of Epic and Pastoral Design, which met during the winter to share experience and recapture memory of wild days in the mountains. Particularly wild was the journey made by Robert Fulke Greville, who in 1792 was travelling in North Wales with the artists Julius Caesar Ibbetson and John 'Warwick' Smith. *A Phaeton in a Thunderstorm*, which Ibbetson painted a few years later, shows 'An Actual Scene' (says the label on the back) on the wild rocky track between Pont Aberglaslyn and Tan y Bwlch. The phaeton has veered at an awkward angle towards the precipice on the right hand side, and Ibbetson shows himself putting a rock behind one of the back wheels. A towering crag looms over the scene, while the driver struggles to control the two plunging horses. The three men were on their way to visit Thomas Johnes at Hafod.

John 'Warwick' Smith, *Hafod House* (1793)

CHAPTER 7

Heavenly Hafod

FOR THE LANDSCAPE tourist, quivering with sensibil-
ity, Hafod could not be missed. Roughly fifteen miles
inland from Aberystwyth, this was the estate into which
Thomas Johnes (1748–1816) poured his life, his love and
all his money. Created from nothing in the wooded hills of
Cardiganshire, it quickly became another object of pilgrimage for those in search of the picturesque ideal. Johnes had
been brought up in the relative comfort of Croft Castle in
Herefordshire, but owned extensive estates in Cardiganshire,
where his family had its roots. Nobody for generations had
bothered about Hafod, or any other of these rundown shabby
lands, hard to reach, hard to make a living from, generally
despised. Johnes's father called Hafod 'a Beggarly estate'.
Riding through the nearby country in the 1770s, the English
traveller Henry Penruddocke Wyndham (1736–1819)
described the mountains as 'more horrible than any we had
seen before. They were of a greater height and larger extent;
while their tops ended in so many various and irregular shapes,
and formed so undulating an horizon, that a warm imagination might almost conceive that the mountains were impelled
and driven on by a supernatural storm, in immense waves and
broken swells.'[1] But when, in the summer of 1780, Johnes
went for the first time to visit his Cardiganshire estates, he
was caught by the extraordinary beauty of the hills around
Hafod. The river Ystwyth thundered in a wildly exhilarating

way through the valley below, and, unlike the bare desolate land that came before and after, the slopes round Hafod were covered with trees. It was untamed. It was awe-inspiring. And it was his.

There had been a house at Hafod probably since Elizabethan times, though no one from his family had lived in it for generations. But one of his Herbert ancestors had planted the trees that surrounded the house, and Johnes, against all reason (and advice), decided that this was where he wanted to be. Turning his back on the well-kept, richly productive land of his Herefordshire estate, Johnes determined to make Hafod his home. At thirty-two he needed a project, and perhaps he was envious of what his cousin, Richard Payne Knight, had achieved at Downton, where he had built a huge and picturesque castle, medieval in inspiration. At Foxley, too, Johnes's great friend Uvedale Price was engaged in creating a heaven on earth, ornamenting Foxley's grounds in the latest picturesque taste with walks and rides and shrubberies and sham ruins. The expense was not counted if the result was a view in the correct aesthetic style.

Commandeering labour from the villages round about, Johnes began his work with a stone wall enclosing the eight square acres that would eventually provide the setting for the house he had yet to build. Miners drafted in from nearby Ysbyty Ystwyth blew up inconvenient rocks and a massive tree-planting programme began. In the five and a half years between October 1795 and April 1801, Johnes planted 2,065,000 trees on his hillsides, including larch (250,000), ash (250,000), birch (80,000), oak (10,000), rowan (10,000), alder (10,000), beech (5,000) and firs (5,000). In June 1786, Johnes's wife, Jane, laid the foundation stone of the house, fantasy Gothic in style, that had been designed for them by Thomas Baldwin of Bath. John Nash, then based in Carmarthen, was probably responsible for the octagonal library that was added to the house in 1793. (Johnes, a passionate bibliophile, was celebrated particularly for his translation of Froissart's chronicles, one of the rare manuscripts in his collection.) No expense was spared in furnishing Hafod – marble fireplaces, Gobelin tapestries, French mirrors – and when the family moved in, Johnes began to lay out picturesque walks in the valley of the Ystwyth, taking in a cold bath, natural caves, an unnatural Alpine bridge and a druid temple – though he does not seem to have employed a druid. Or a hermit, a fashionable figure on eighteenth-century estates of this nature. Encouraged by his friend, Uvedale Price, who in 1794 had begun to publish his influential *Essays on the Picturesque*, Johnes would have been aware of the prevailing aesthetic, and the principle of creating landscape pictures to be viewed from fixed points in the perambulation around the estate. A 'correctly' educated landscaper knew how to 'help' the landscape to show off its best features. A correctly educated traveller knew how he ought to look, though Johnes could not always depend on his visitors to look at Hafod in the 'right' way. The topographer Benjamin Heath Malkin declared, 'the circumstances are eccentric and wonderful, but not picturesque. There is neither foliage nor herbage; nothing but rock and water, confined as it were in one of nature's cabins.'[2]

Malkin, though, was in a minority. Visitors flocked to Hafod, so many that Johnes built the Hafod Arms at nearby Devil's Bridge to provide convenient overnight accommodation. Tickets for tours of the estate could be bought from the landlord. As MP for Cardiganshire (and later its Lord Lieutenant), and a well-known collector of manuscripts and antiquities, the hospitable Johnes had a wide acquaintance, including the King's equerry, Robert Fulke Greville, who in 1792 had had such a tempestuous journey on his way to Hafod. Greville, a younger son of the Earl of Warwick, stayed at Hafod with Ibbetson, who had begun life as a ship painter in Hull, and John 'Warwick' Smith (1749–1831), who got his nickname because it was the Earl who established his career. Smith's watercolour of the cobwebby Gothic house shows it in the middle distance, smoke from a chimney rising against wooded hills, with undulating parkland sweeping down to the river in which cattle are cooling their hocks. His watercolours were later transformed into aquatints to illustrate James Edward Smith's book, *Fifteen Views Illustrative of a Tour to Hafod in Cardiganshire*, published in 1810, which sold for the astounding price of twelve guineas.

Among the fifteen illustrations was a view of the celebrated Cavern Cascade at Hafod – rocks, waterfalls, blasted trees hanging out over the ravine, a seemingly insecure wooden bridge spanning the chasm. 'Words are totally insufficient to express all the varied effect of the river broken by projecting cliffs,' wrote Smith, 'the craggy valley, the overshadowing trees, the rich amphitheatre of woody hills in the more distant prospect, and the towering mountains that bound the whole. This is a complete composition, a picture which surely no critic would presume to correct.'[3] James Edward Smith (1759–1828) was the great naturalist who, on the death of the famous Swedish botanist, Carl Linnaeus, bought his collection for a thousand guineas (borrowed from his doubtful wool-merchant father), transferred it to England and with it founded the Linnean Society. He and Johnes corresponded over a long period and Smith stayed at Hafod several times.

Another intriguing set of views of the Hafod landscape exist on the remaining pieces of a superb dessert service of Derby china which Johnes ordered in June 1787.[4] Had he perhaps seen the vast china service commissioned by Catherine, the Empress of Russia, from the Wedgwood factory, decorated with views of 'picturesque landscapes of

Great Britain', a sensation when it was exhibited in London in 1774? The Hafod scenes – 'The Menagerie' on a beautiful heart-shaped dish; 'A View West from Cefn Coch overlooking the Cow Meadow'; 'The Ystwyth near the old foot bridge' – are different from those engraved for Smith's book, and glow in gold-bordered medallions set in the centre of the various dishes with their dark blue borders. Who made the original paintings from which these views were taken, and which no longer seem to exist? Was it Richard Wilson's most brilliant pupil, Thomas Jones, who showed paintings of Hafod at the Royal Academy in 1786?[5]

Writers were as entranced with the place as painters, and Johnes, writing to George Cumberland (1754–1848) to congratulate him on his *Poems on Landscapes*, invited the poet to stay. The result was *An Attempt to Describe Hafod* (1796) written two years after his visit. 'No language can image out the sublimity of the scenes;' says Cumberland, 'which, without quite arriving at a sentiment of aversion, produces, in the empassioned soul, all those thrilling sensations of terror, which ever arise from majestical, yet gloomy exhibitions.'[6] His book included a folding map of part of the Hafod estate, engraved by William Blake, whose book *Songs of Innocence* was in the Hafod library. Blake shows the river curving through from the top right to the bottom left of the map, the steep contours of the hills either side and the principal features of the landscape Johnes created: the lake, various bridges across the river, clusters of cottages, the picturesque paths that wound through the estate. Annotated on the map are the page numbers relating to Cumberland's description. And was Turner there? In homage to Richard Wilson, he made a tour of Wales in 1798 and left a gorgeous watercolour of a house in a setting that's roughly right and that in its pinnacled, battlemented Gothic style is also roughly right. But the details don't quite match. It's a chimera, like the dream that Johnes always held on to, that here, in his Cardiganshire redoubt, he could create a paradise that was not only beautiful but productive and useful too.

Johnes poured three inherited fortunes into Hafod and the money travelled only in one direction, since he was not only wildly extravagant, but also idealistic. His estate, he declared, should be a model community, where contented tenants lived in dry cottages, farming the land in the most modern and productive way. Improvement was the thing just then, with Thomas Coke's experiments going on at Holkham and the establishment of the Board of Agriculture in 1793. And so in September 1795, when he had already been living at Hafod for seven years, Johnes invited the eminent agriculturist Dr James Anderson to advise on ways to farm the land more efficiently. At that time, it was as important for a landowner to be seen to be au fait with the latest agricultural practices as it was for him to lay out the grounds round his house in the latest style and fashion. At Woburn, the fifth Duke of Bedford became famous for the annual sheep shearings he held on his estate, the fore-runner of the agricultural shows of today (the Bath and West Show was set up in 1777). Huge numbers of people gathered to watch ploughing matches, competitions for hedging and ditching, demonstrations of the latest agricultural machinery, guided tours of the Duke's arable fields, inspections of prize rams and bulls. The gathering was open to all who had interest enough to come (and the means to travel to Bedfordshire) and all were fed and watered. When the Duke died, Johnes set up an obelisk at Hafod in his memory. The inscription commem-orated the Duke not as a nobleman or a statesman, but as a 'Friend of Agriculture'.

And so Anderson arrived to try to turn the thin, hungry, too-wet soils of Cardiganshire into ground that would provide waving fields of corn, and fat, productive cattle. From the beginning Johnes had tried. He had made pasture where there had been bog. He had created woods where there had been bare moorland. They looked very beautiful. But even he could not escape from the unpleasant reflection that, as another agricultural commentator of the time had written, 'The gratification of the eye was purchased at too high a price, by excluding the operation of the plough and the scythe from the spot where it grew, thereby lessening the more substantial and the more requisite comforts of society, by lessening the means of subsistence.'[7]

Johnes had not yet been able to persuade his land to yield an income. And even he, with his supreme gift of seeing only what he wanted to see, was beginning to realise that his fortune was disappearing at an alarming rate. He had always boasted that he could turn Hafod into an estate that paid its way. Anderson, a Scot, recently lauded for his work in Aberdeenshire, where he had reclaimed vast tracts of barren mountain and brought it into profitable cultivation, was not daunted by the Hafod land. He thought it had potential. Bringing Johnes's tenants round to his point of view was an entirely more complex proposition. They and their families had been scratching a living from this land for generations before Johnes arrived with his grand schemes and rosy visions. They had no reserves to fall back on if things went disastrously wrong. It was safer, all round, to stick to what they knew.

Nevertheless, that first autumn, Johnes rode with Anderson round the Hafod estate, delighted with Anderson's response to the beauty of the place, with the trees in the valleys beginning to turn from green to russet, but also heartened to hear the views of the first man, besides himself, to believe that the place could be persuaded into profit. Anyone trying to make money from the land in Cardiganshire was starting from a low base. The wheeled cart was only just beginning to replace the wooden sledges, the *car llus* pulled by oxen that was a familiar sight all over the hillier parts of Wales. On steep, rough ground, it was considered a safer, more stable way of carrying loads than a cart. The Welsh plough, to which all farmers remained intractably attached, was described by an official sent down from the newly founded Board of Agriculture as 'perhaps the most awkward, unmeaning tool to be found in any civilised country; it is not calculated to cut a furrow, but to tear it open by main force.' The indigenous Welsh inhabitants, seen by the tourists of landscape as agreeably exotic, romantic even in their role as the last of the ancient Britons driven west by the invading Romans, gave quite a different impression if you actually lived among them. They were suspicious of strangers, especially ones who kept telling them what to do.

They had no money, so they farmed with what they had. They carted seaweed from the shore to manure their land (and in believing in its efficacy, they were quite right). They did without lime, because that would have to be paid for. One of the biggest problems, the one that kept most farming at no more than subsistence level, was the county's isolation from markets for their produce. Boats came into Aberystwyth from London but it was a long journey, too long for perishable products. Bacon and salted butter could be sold in Bristol, but even that was several days away, with a laden pony. Cattle were usually delivered into the hands of drovers, who took them on immensely long journeys, with high casualty rates, cross-country to the great cattle fairs in Kent and Essex. At Hafod, Johnes had built a model dairy in which his wife, Jane, took a great interest. They produced tons of cheese there – Cheddar, Parmesan and Stilton – but even Johnes, with all his energy, all his contacts, couldn't find a sale for his model cheeses and ended up giving them to his tenants. The tenants wouldn't even use the Swansea pottery vessels that Johnes urged on them, as a more hygienic alternative to their wooden ones. Pottery could break. The milk might be lost. Wood was more reliable.

But he never stopped trying to bring about that vision, of a place equally to be praised for its productivity as its beauty. In 1784, before he had even begun to build his new house at Hafod, he had been one of the founders of a local Society for the Encouragement of Agriculture and Industry, typical of the kind of philanthropically motivated societies being set up all over the country. But in Cardiganshire it did not flourish, and by 1796, the year in which Johnes's wife laid the foundation stone of his Gothic fantasy, subscriptions had dried up and the society had petered out.

Johnes built immaculate milking parlours and magnificent stables at Hafod and invited his tenants to see for themselves the advantages of housing animals properly and feeding them well. But perhaps he never quite grasped the irony of the fact that the few farmers who turned up (perhaps for the free beer) lived in conditions very much less palatial than the stock they had been summoned to admire. He brought in models of the new ploughs that were now being invented at a great rate, tested them on the hillsides of the estate and employed black-smiths to make copies of the ones that coped best with the uncompromising terrain. These he offered as encouragement, free, to any tenant who, like him, dreamed of improvement. There were very few.

He had the resources (or persuaded himself he had) to drain boggy land. He had the cash to buy lime to sweeten its acidity. But if he'd ever actually sat down to calculate the true cost of the potatoes and corn that came from this reclaimed ground, he might have seen that the expenditure in labour, let alone materials, was completely beyond the average tenant. Instead, his own example not proving quite enough to galvanise them, he imported several poor Scottish families to take on some of his farms in North Cardiganshire and demonstrate what thrift and industry could wring from the land. Johnes had a high regard for the Scots. His head forester, John Greenshields, was Scottish. So was his head gardener, James Todd, who came to Hafod from the botanic garden at Edinburgh. From the north of England, he brought down an expert ploughman to show what fantastic miracles could be wrought from the new Rotherham plough. The Cardiganshire farmers were not impressed.

In 1801, he dreamed up a scheme to bring a hundred families from Grisons in Switzerland to Hafod and to lease them 7,500 acres of particularly barren mountain. The deal was that they could have it at a rent of 1/6 an acre for three 'lives' and Johnes evidently had no doubt that very quickly his Swiss migrants would create the ideal communities that his Cardiganshire tenants had so persistently failed to deliver. They would tame the wilderness, bring forth harvests where there had previously been none. It would be a shining example for all other landowners to emulate. But the expense involved in bringing over the Swiss farmers was considerable and Johnes applied to the Prime Minister, Henry Addington, to advance 'the 100 families £10,000 for the expenses of travelling etc.' There was a great deal bound up in that 'etc.' Addington turned down the proposal.

Instead Johnes turned to his pen, producing *A Cardiganshire Landlord's Advice to his Tenants*, and distributed copies free – with a Welsh translation.[8] 'That nothing may be wanting on my part to promote a better system of cultivation,' he wrote, 'I intend having your farms inspected; and giving to those who have managed their farms in the best manner such implements of husbandry as may encourage them to proceed, in so praiseworthy a track.' He quoted his advisor, James Anderson, who had published a good many articles on the proper management of land, crops and stock. He quoted one of the great writers on agriculture, Arthur Young, who had begun to publish his *Annals of Agriculture* in 1784. He pointed out the advantages of a proper rotation of crops, a subject on which Charles Townshend of Raynham Hall in Norfolk had done so much research. His Hafod tenants mostly grew oats in the same ground, year after year; harvests diminished as the same nutrients in the ground were progressively exhausted. 'In all the leases I grant,' continued Johnes imperiously, 'there will be a clause to prevent this destructive practice from being continued, which shall be religiously kept; on the contrary, I shall not forget to reward those who follow a better system.' He was like a parent trying to persuade a child that greens were good for it.

Like sweets, those rewards did the trick, at least temporarily. There were premiums, cash prizes, gold medals for tenants who followed the 'advice', all paid for by Thomas Johnes. Johnes himself was awarded several gold medals in recognition of his services to farming and forestry. And year in, year out, he continued his own experiments, bringing in forty Friesian cows from Holland as part of a trial to find out the best kind of milking cattle for his particular ground. Visiting Hafod in the autumn of 1799, Richard Cumberland, a farming vicar from Driffield in Gloucestershire, pronounced the dairy 'the best I ever saw', but still the cheese – five tons of it – stacked up unsold. Despite Dr Anderson's guiding hand, Hafod refused to produce a profit, but writing to Cumberland in 1804, Anderson marvelled at Johnes's undaunted spirit. He 'talks of Hafod as a paradise, and of his improvements with rapture, as if he had never met with a single disappointment in his life'.[9] Only his trees did well, especially the larch, which was well suited to life on the cold, exposed flanks of the hills. But the trees were a long-term crop. And the way he looked at them, they were scarcely a crop at all, for he had planted them primarily to bring even more beauty to the landscape around Hafod. They went in the end, but not until after Johnes, heartbroken at the loss of his only child, had died in April 1816. Hafod's extraordinary renown, its reputation as the pinnacle of picturesque beauty, had lasted for no more than twenty-five years. No one ever again cared about it as much as Johnes, its passionate creator. In September 1832 creditors, who included Johnes's wine merchant, forced the sale of the estate, together with the house and all its contents. Hafod, which for a short period in the early nineteenth century had been thought of as an earthly paradise, an Eden, was sold off for £70,000 to the Duke of Newcastle, who never lived there. The last owner, a Mr Waddingham, walked out in the 1930s. In 1956 the house was blown up. But the setting remains: the hills, the streams, the rushing river that exerted such a strange, strong pull on Johnes. In the undergrowth hover the remains of his serpentine walks, whispering of their ghosts.

PART TWO

PROSPECTS AND THE PLOUGH

We may talke what we please of Lilies
and Lions Rampant and Spread Eagles in
Fields d'Or or d'Argent; but if Heraldry
Were guided by Reason, a Plough in a Field
Arable would be the most Noble and Antient Armes.

Abraham Cowley, *Of Agriculture* (1650)

Samuel Palmer, *The Early Ploughman* (c. 1861)

CHAPTER 8

The Board of Agriculture

HAFOD DID NOT feature in the report that Thomas
Lloyd, Esq., and the Revd Mr Turnor wrote for
the Board of Agriculture giving their *General View
of the Agriculture of the County of Cardigan* in 1794. They
would have approved, no doubt, of Johnes's enthusiasm for
'improving', but they were a year too early to see the start
of the massive programme of tree planting and development
that he embarked on in 1795. While painters, writers (and
tourists in their wake) travelled through the landscapes of
Britain distilling their experiences into a series of single
impressions – the landscape stopped at one moment in
time – another band of men, the agriculturists, the farmers,
the improvers were travelling with a completely different
aim. And so, the year after Gainsborough painted *The Harvest
Wagon,* Arthur Young published the first of his remarkable
commentaries on the state of agricultural England, his *Six
Weeks' Tour Through the Southern Counties* (1768). In the year
that William Gilpin made his tour down the River Wye, with
the aim of 'examining the face of a country *by the rules of
picturesque beauty*', the indefatigable Arthur Young was making
his *Six Months' Tour Through the North of England*, looking at
the country with a very different aim in view. By 1771, the
year that Paul Sandby toured North Wales in the company of
his patron, Sir Watkin Williams-Wynn, Young was in Suffolk
and Norfolk, gathering material for his *Farmer's Tour Through*

the East of England. Five years later, while Sandby oversaw the publication of his *XII Views in North Wales*, Arthur Young was assessing the agricultural state of Shropshire. The year before Thomas West brought out his bestselling *Guide* to the Lake District, with its precise instructions on how to look at the views that mattered, a small group of prosperous farmers got together in Somerset to found the Bath and West show. In 1783, as Thomas Gainsborough set off to paint in the Lake District, Robert Bakewell (1725–1795) set up the Dishley Society. Bakewell, born at Dishley Grange, near Loughborough in Leicestershire, was the first person to breed farm animals systematically, with a particular aim in view. Selecting from sheep with particularly good fleeces, he produced the Lincoln Longwool. Using a Westmorland bull, he bred the first cattle to be raised primarily for beef rather than milk. Lord Ribblesdale, for whom James Ward painted his immense canvas of the sublime, *A Landscape, Gordale Scar, Yorkshire*, was surely as interested in the provenance and breeding of the great white bull that Ward set so prominently in the foreground of his picture, as he was in the landscape against which it is set. The same bull – Ward calls it the 'Adonis' of the scene – stars in the foreground of the view Ward made of the *Lake and Tower in De Tabley Park*, Sir John Leicester's Cheshire seat.

And so they continued to flip, these two sides of the landscape coin, throughout the late eighteenth and the early nineteenth century. Arthur Young's *Annals of Agriculture* coincided with Gilpin's *Observations* on the Lake District. As Uvedale Price was publishing his elegant *Essays on the Picturesque* (1794–6), Arthur Young was scanning the first of the *General Views* on the agriculture of England and Wales commissioned from 1793 onwards. The artists came away from their journeys with landscapes captured in sketchbooks and on canvases. The

agricultural reformers were engaging with something different – a process, not a product. They were attempting to chart
and comment on a never-ending calendar of things done or
not done on the land, crops grown, soils ameliorated (or not),
incomes earned, patterns of employment, methods of deal-
ing with the land which varied enormously from county to
county. The variation was not in itself surprising, for farming
had to follow the capabilities of the land. In the rich counties of central England, there would be more arable than in
the west country, where the landscape was dominated by the
grassy pastures of the great chalk sheep runs. Inevitably, the
reports varied widely in their coverage, and in the degree
to which the different writers identified with the neighbour-
hood and (more rarely) its inhabitants.

There had been earlier reports of course, other journeys –
Celia Fiennes, Daniel Defoe – but the focus on looking at
the landscape primarily through its farming activities inten-
sified from the middle of the eighteenth century, largely
due to the writings of Arthur Young and William Marshall.
Marshall, one of the great agricultural commentators of
the time, was a Yorkshireman, born into a farming family
in the North Riding. By the age of thirty, he was managing
a farm at Addiscombe in Surrey and it was this experience that provided the material for his first book *Minutes
of Agriculture made on a farm of three hundred acres of various
soils near Croydon . . . published as a sketch of the actual business of a farm* (1778). The title suggests Marshall's strengths.
He knew what he was talking about, the actual business.
But he was opinionated, and the positions he held, as agent
to various landowners, never lasted long. He fell out with
Sir Harbord Harbord at Gunton in Norfolk; he quarrelled
with Samuel Pipe-Wolferstan at Statfold, near Tamworth.
But none of his experiences were wasted. *The Rural Economy*

of Norfolk (1787) was the first of six important studies that Marshall made of agricultural practices in different parts of the country, covering Yorkshire (1788), Gloucestershire (1789), the Midlands (1790), the west country (1796) and finishing with his *The Rural Economy of the Southern Counties* in 1798, the year that Wordsworth published 'Tintern Abbey'. In effect, he had invented the series of reports that the Board of Agriculture subsequently began to commission. He had even been the first to propose – in his *Rural Economy of the Midland Counties* – that such a Board be set up, an idea that William Pitt the Younger quickly put into practice in 1793. So you might suppose that when the new Board needed a Secretary to work under its President, Sir John Sinclair, Marshall would get the job. Instead, it went to his older rival, Arthur Young, another indefatigable traveller, observer and asker of questions.

A portrait of Young painted by John Russell when Young was forty-eight, shows a thin-faced, lively-looking man with white hair swept back and dramatically defined eyebrows. The lips are full, the chin long and pointed. The portrait suggests a man with a commanding presence and eyes that missed very little. He was fifty-two when he came to the Board and had already published an extraordinary number of books on agriculture. His method was different from Marshall's. Leaving his home at Bradfield in Suffolk, he swept up information on the hoof, advertising his journeys in the local newspapers of the areas he intended to visit and arranging to meet agents, landowners, stock breeders, experimenters as he passed through. Wherever he was, in Hertfordshire or Essex or Yorkshire, certain themes emerged again and again in his writing: big farms were more sensible than little ones; enclosure was an essential preliminary to improving the standard of agriculture; waste land was a waste and should be brought into cultivation.

He was on the side of the experimenters, not the play-safers. Many people came to visit him at Bradfield, but not all were impressed by what they saw. 'People that devote their time to writing cannot act or execute,' concluded the Northumbrian breeder, George Culley. 'His sheep are scabbed, his cattle ill chose and worse managed, in short he exhibits a sad picture of mismanagement.'¹ But he had friends where it mattered. And he was a more emollient character than the generally splenetic Marshall. So he got the Secretary's job.

Before it could make any recommendations to the government, the Board, set up in the year that France declared war on Britain, the year that John Clare was born and Gilbert White died, first had to learn what was going on in the fifty-four counties of England and Wales. From 1793 onwards, a detailed series of reports flooded in to the Board's London headquarters. The people who had been commissioned to prepare them were of a particular kind – land agents, prosperous farmers – with a particular view of what the land was for. They were pro-landowner, pro-enclosure. The possibilities of land reclamation, drainage, the advantages of better roads and canals, better ploughs and other farm implements, better crops, were never far from their minds. Land was to be used to the best possible advantage of the country as a whole, 'improved', rationalised to maximise profits and to use labour in the most efficient way. Implicit in the reports was a connection between cultivated land and a civilised society. Typical of the commentators were John Billingsley, a landowner who lived on the Mendips at Ashwick Grove, near Shepton Mallet, and who wrote the *General View* of Somerset, and Abraham and William Driver, who in 1794 submitted their *General View of the Agriculture of the County of Hampshire*. 'We are sorry to observe such immense tracts of open heath, and uncultivated land,' they wrote 'which . . . reminds the traveller of uncivilised

nations, where nature pursues her own course, without the
assistance of human art.'²

James Donaldson, who contributed his *General View of the
Agriculture of the County of Northampton* to the Board in 1794,
commended the farmers of the county for making the most of
its natural advantages. 'The surface of this county is as peculiarly
advantageous for cultivation, as it is delightful and ornamen-
tal,' he wrote. 'In no other part of the kingdom, perhaps, are
more agreeable and extensive landscapes to be seen. Here,
there are no dreary wastes, nor rugged and unsightly mountains to offend the eye, or to intercept the view. The surface is
nowhere so irregular, but it can be applied to every purpose of
husbandry and tillage. Every hill is cultivated, or may be kept
in a profitable state of pasturage, and every inequality in the
surface contributes to its ornament and beauty.'³

In writing about Cardiganshire, Thomas Lloyd and the
Reverend Turnor felt they had constantly to apologise for the
unimproved wastes and wildness that existed, particularly in
the north and east of the county. Thomas Johnes, of course,
responded in an entirely different way to this essential characteristic of the landscape. He loved its wild energy, though he
also wanted to change it, create an exemplary estate in which
usefulness and beauty could be held in perfect equilibrium.
He was unusual in that respect, balanced between two ideals,
so different in their nature. But Lloyd and Turnor had a clear
brief and it was resolutely set out in the title page – not only a
General View of the Agriculture of the county but also *Observations
on the Means of its Improvement*.

They were, at least, knowledgeable commentators, for both
had land in the county; Lloyd wrote about the southern half,
Turnor covered the wilder north. Some of the best land was
fast disappearing, they wrote, as the Irish Sea encroached on
the barley-growing areas of the western coast. But even on the

best land, explained Lloyd, little attempt was made to feed it with manure or practise the rotation of crops that Charles 'Turnip' Townshend had proved to be so profitable on his land at Raynham Hall, Norfolk in the 1730s. Each individual farmer pursued his own method (probably with good reason, I feel inclined to mutter). 'I am sorry', writes Lloyd, 'that truth compels me, to make such a report to your board, of the agriculture of this county.' The ploughs were 'too bad for description'. The county had 'but little wood, and that little is daily lessening'. But they did have an Agriculture Society (the society of which Thomas Johnes became a founder member in 1774) and Lloyd was sure that this would eventually 'excite a spirit of improvement, in a people naturally so shrewd and sensible as the natives of Cardigan'.[4]

Lloyd describes the field boundaries, made from alternating layers of sod and long stones, typically 5 ft high and perhaps 7 ft wide at the base. These grassy boundaries, thick in summer with toadflax and blue scabious, are still a characteristic feature of the low lands in the western counties of Wales. But they would not contain sheep, who scrambled over them in pursuit of better pasture. Managing sheep was impossible, Turnor pointed out, because of the 'total want of materials for hurdles within a proper distance'.[5] The thick stands of coppiced hazel that are still such a feature of the landscape in counties such as Hampshire and Dorset made sheepfolds possible and profitable, too, since the flock manured the land while they were folded inside the home-made hazel hurdles.

To a far greater degree than other commentators – and almost certainly because they lived among them – Lloyd and Turnor described the appalling conditions in which agricultural labourers worked and the impossibility of their managing to live on the low wages that were then routinely paid: sixpence (£40.91 in today's money) a week from October to

Candlemas, eightpence (£54.01) a week for the rest, when the working day stretched from five in the morning till seven at night. 'Their pay bears no proportion to the price of provisions, or the labour they perform,' wrote Lloyd, who must have known that this was not what the Board of Agriculture wanted to hear.[6] Because of the shortage of wooded areas, turf was the most common fuel, but it had to be carted from a distance (and Lloyd estimated that the average family needed at least six loads a year). Without money, the poorest people paid for fuel with their labour – four days' harvest work for each load – but that meant forgoing their wages. As more land was brought into cultivation in the county, there were fewer places where labourers could gather furze to augment the expensively carted turf.

The tone in the *General View* for Caernarvonshire was markedly different.[7] George Kay, who wrote it, showed little sympathy with the labourers of the county, of whom, he noted, 'a great number are methodists'. He particularly deplored the fact that, 'If an itinerant preacher comes into the country, who generally preaches on the high ways, they walk off, and leave their work, to the great detriment of their masters.'[8] But those same labourers had contracted for lower wages in return for the freedom to attend methodist meetings. Kay, though, was a Scot, from Leith. He didn't understand. And he had evidently had a hard time getting anybody to talk to him, suspicious as they must have been of his intentions.

Kay knew he hadn't done a good job in North Wales, the whole of which became his remit when he stepped in at the last minute to replace the Board's first appointee. In an unusual step, he prefaced his report with an open letter to its President, Sir John Sinclair, outlining the difficulties he had faced. The biggest problem lay in the fact that he'd not been able to get a map of the area, not even in Edinburgh. He arrived late in the season, when travelling had become difficult. Then, 'In some instances, no opportunity was allowed me, either of showing or explaining the plan of the board; and when it was, I sometimes found gentlemen averse from the scheme.'⁹ If, that is, the gentlemen could even understand the scheme. Most of the farmers in North Wales spoke only Welsh, and even if they understood English might well have chosen not to reveal the fact.

Only in his introduction to Caernarvonshire, 'the most rugged and truly Alpine' of all the counties of North Wales, does Kay briefly mention Snowdon, and the wild scenery that had inspired Richard Wilson and so many other artists – Ibbetson, Girtin, Turner, Paul Sandby. Penmaenmawr, which had provided the dramatic setting for William Williams's painting *Thunderstorm with the Death of Amelia* (1784), was, he said, 'a most tremendous mountain'. From here, a rugged precipice dropped down to the sea with a road cut through the rock for the mail coaches travelling between London and Holyhead. Describing the route, Kay begins to sound less like the hard-nosed Scots surveyor, and more like the travellers who came to North Wales in search of landscapes to inspire (it was, after all, one of the prime destinations). 'The road is perfectly secure,' wrote Kay, 'but the loose impending rocks from above present an awful appearance, threatening to fall down, and crush the traveller below.'¹⁰ But, writing of Merionethshire, he showed no susceptibility to the grandeur of Cader Idris, or the dark waters of the pool below, made famous by Richard Wilson's painting. For Joseph Hucks, who was touring North Wales with his friend Samuel Taylor Coleridge at almost exactly the same time as Kay, Cader Idris was a sublime experience: 'When I stood upon the edge of this precipice and looked into the frightful abyss of clouds, it put me in mind of the chaos, or void space of darkness, so finely described in Milton, where the fallen archangel stood at the gates of hell, pondering the scene before him and viewing with horror the profound expanse of silence and eternal night.'[11] Kay, though acknowledging Cader (he spelt it Kader) Idris as the highest mountain in Merionethshire, noted only that Tallyllyn, at the foot of the mountain, was the best place in the county to go for rams.

Nevertheless, not all those practical men, riding through the country from Cornwall to Kent, from Hampshire to Cumberland and Westmorland, were blind to the beauty of what they were seeing. John Billingsley, who wrote the *General View* of Somerset in 1794, commented on the 'romantick and picturesque' appearance of the woods in the county. Charles Hassall, who compiled the *General View* of Carmarthenshire (he lived at Eastwood, near Narberth), wrote glowingly of the Vale of Towy where 'a few hills raise their heads to a considerable elevation, from whose summits the beauties of the Vale are viewed to great advantage; Grongar Hill and the venerable ruins of Dynevor Castle, are situations from which the eye is delighted by the richest prospects the imagination can form.'[12] Writing their *General View* of Cumberland, which took in a good part of the Lake District, John Bailey and George Culley were unusually susceptible to 'the height, ruggedness, steepness of the sides (in some places ornamented with wood and projecting rocks), the varied forms, sublime assemblage, and picturesque beauty of these mountains, and the lakes they environ, [which] form scenes that few other places, if any, in the island can equal; and have at different times exercised the pens of many descriptive writers.' Sublime! Picturesque! You can almost hear the bit biting as the authors rein themselves in and comment, more soberly, that the slate of the mountains was 'deservedly esteemed for covering the roofs of houses'. These places they observed, 'with their pleasing accompaniments, have of late years made the tour of the lakes a fashionable amusement, from whence considerable emoluments have resulted to the neighbouring inhabitants'.[13]

The first editions of the *General Views* were published, stitched but not bound, on sheets of paper 10 in x 8 in, with margins two and a half inches wide either side of the text. The idea was to distribute the accounts to different people within the various counties who might have views on the subjects covered. There was a general invitation to pencil comments in the margins and return the reports to the Board. There was a strongly patriotic note in the advertisement at the beginning of each report, which reminded readers that, 'There is no Circumstance from which any one can derive more real Satisfaction, than that of contributing, by every possible means, to promote the Improvement of his Country.' The Board of Agriculture counted among its honorary members several dukes (Bedford, Buccleuch and Grafton) as well as prominent, forward-looking landowners such as Thomas Coke of Holkham in Norfolk. Each of the members was presented with a diploma illustrated with a view and an accompanying description:

The landscape is intended to represent the view of a country, the greater part of which is already recovered from an unprofitable state into various and beneficial cultivation; the grounds immediately on the banks of the river are supposed to be rich meadows, rendered fertile by the judicious application of the water which passes through them; the foreground scene, extending to the hills, is principally occupied with the various branches of tillage: on one side of the river, cultivation is brought to perfection, and plantations, scattered everywhere, enrich the scene; on the other, the summit of the hill is uncultivated, but appropriated to pasture, and

covered with sheep. The whole is designed to comprehend
the leading objects of improved husbandry; the picture is
supported by a male and female figure, representing the
distinct characters of rural labours, with their respective
attributes.[14]

Meadows efficiently watered, arable land properly tilled,
woods planted, sheep profitably pastured: this was the Board
of Agriculture's vision of a perfect landscape.

Comments on the first draft of the *General Views* were to be
addressed to the President of the Board of Agriculture, Sir John
Sinclair, Bart, MP. These were collated and incorporated into
new editions of the reports which began to appear from 1805
to 1817. The men who wrote these remarkable reports were
marked out by, indeed almost certainly chosen for, a particular point of view. The *General View of Agriculture in the County of
Wiltshire* (1794) was written by Thomas Davis, steward to Lord
Bath at Longleat. John Claridge, who wrote the *General View* of
Dorset, had had twenty years' experience 'in the cultivation
and management of landed property in the county'. James
Donaldson, who compiled the report on Northamptonshire,
was, like the other reporters, a forward-looking man, focused
on productivity. Their Recommendations for Improvements
concentrated on topics such as cultivating waste land, drainage, improving strains of oats and other crops, bringing in
better breeds of cattle and sheep.

These were four of the improvements recommended by
John Holt, surveying the state of agriculture in the county of
Lancaster, on the western edge of the Lake District.[15] He was
engaged to write about agriculture, not the landscape of the
region, but, as in all the reports, a particular picture built up
of what the place looked like at this time (1795). Lancashire,
unlike most of the counties being surveyed, was fully in
the throes of the Industrial Revolution. It was a landscape

dominated by factories, not agriculture. Spinners, bleachers, weavers, dyers, printers, tool-makers were more commonly to be met with than field labourers. Of the two unsavoury labour markets open to them, workers preferred the factories, wrote Holt, 'where they may work by the piece and under cover'. The Sankey Canal had opened in 1757, connecting St Helens with the Mersey River and making it easier to bring coal from the Lancashire mines to the factories of Liverpool. Holt noted the considerable effect that 'the many canals already begun, and intended' had had 'both upon the agriculture, manufactures, and general state of the country'. A map at the front of the report showed the different terrains of the county: the craggy mountains of lime and freestone, with its 'woody declivities and fertile vales' that ran inland from Furness; the 'fertile plain' of the Fylde; the moss and the waste lands 'yet capable of improvement'. The mosses and fens alone, he estimated, covered 26,500 acres, an area almost as big as Bedfordshire. He pointed out the amount of pasture needed as bleaching ground for the cottons produced in the factories, and the unusually small amount of sheep, which he put down to the number of dogs kept by people in the fast-growing urban areas of the county. He notes the huge flocks of geese brought, on a certain day, from different parts of the county to be turned out on Martin Mere. 'These flocks are so marked, as again to be known. Upon this Mere they continue till about Michaelmas, and on this water they can find sufficient of food for their sustenance from the different grasses, aquatics, fishes and insects. The proprietor of the water claims half of the flock that remains alive for their summer's keep.'

Passed over by the Board of Agriculture, Marshall's revenge on his rival Young came in the form of the five volumes of *The Review and Abstracts of the County Reports to the Board of Agriculture* (1818), the making of which occupied the final

nine years of his life. He rearranged the Board's reports by
region, which he felt was a far more useful way of looking at
the country than the more artificial divisions of counties. He
took great pleasure in pointing out the inadequacies of some
of the authors. But the best thing about the abstracts was the
opportunity it gave him to have the last word. As he shall have
here, with his notes (almost as though he were speaking into
a tape recorder) on a landscape between South Molton and
Dulverton in North Devonshire, which he rode through on
Thursday 18 September 1794 (a distance of thirteen miles)
and which he describes so minutely, you could paint it.

Exmore, in this point of view, is without feature; appears as
a flat, or at most, a tamely billowing heath. Its hills scarcely
rise above the cultivated swells that environ them. This side
of it, at least, has a not a trait of the Mountain character.

Wind along the brink of the valley. The opposite banks
apparently well soiled and well cultivated; though they form
the immediate skirts or margins of the Moor.

Some wooded dells branch out of the valley.

Sheep on these Commons, similar to those of West Devonshire and Cornwall! Part horned; part hornless.

See corn in arrish mows; or small field stacks.

Trace a ridge of cold land: a woodland soil; and leave a
similar dip to the right.

Enter and skirt a wide fern-grown Common: large plots
of fern now in swath. Also dwarf furze and some heath. The
soil deep and culturable.

Approach still nearer the Exmore Heaths: now crimsoned
with blossoms; which brighten as the day clears up.

The soil of the Moor Skirts somewhat red.

Laid out in a large square Danmonian Fields. Much of it
in a state of arable land: a few Turneps.

The valley widens, and breaks in well soiled hillocks. The two parishes of East and West Anstey appear to be in a good state of culture. Several plowed fields; apparently clean fallows.

Meet strings of Lime Horses; from Bampton Lime Works.

Several instances of good young Cattle, of the North Devon breed.

Building materials . . . Earth and Thatch: an entire suite of new Farm Buildings, just finished, of these materials.

Lose sight of the Exmore Hills; but still keep the brink of the valley; having enjoyed a tolerably level road for seven or eight miles!

Holly abounds in this cold situation: it is seen to mix frequently with the Alder.

Leave the high ground, and descend into the valley. Subsoil slatey rubble.

Stirring Wheat Fallows, with four oxen: the first oxen, and the first plow, I have seen at work, in North Devonshire!

The road, of black Limestone, is narrow but well laid out.

Thick polled Sheep, as in the South Hams.

Instance of watering Grassland: the first I have observed, in North Devonshire.

'Dunstone', and good Grassland, as about Moulton.

A Lime kiln: black stone, lodged among 'Dunstone'.

Some tolerably large Orchards; with low Devonshire trees; though within the County of Somerset.

Another Sea, or rather another Bay, of rich Danmonian swells.

Approach Dulverton; by another Gothic bridge.[16]

15 45/150   Reynolds Stone

Reynolds Stone, *Dorset Landscape*, from *The Old Rectory* (1976)

CHAPTER 9

William Cobbett

THE REVISIONS OF the Board of Agriculture's *General Views* were pretty much complete by 1817, but the process of evaluating the land in terms of its agricultural potential was greatly enlivened by William Cobbett (1763–1835), whose reports of his *Rural Rides* started to appear in 1821, in the pages of his journal, the *Political Register*. His first ride took him from London to Gloucester, by way of Newbury, Marlborough and Cirencester. He made his last ride, from Kensington into Hampshire, in August 1826.

Cobbett rode with the eyes of a yeoman farmer, constantly appraising the capabilities of the land he was passing through. He appreciated well-grown crops, well-tended orchards, properly managed flocks. He was fantastically energetic, endlessly curious, splenetic, endearing in his lack of self-doubt. Where Gilpin saw pictures to be painted, Cobbett saw swedes. If only farmers would do things his way, sow more swedes, and sow that seed in drills rather than broadcast, then agriculture in Britain might yet be saved. 'Cobbett's Quackeries', his enemies called these obsessions – for American corn (the maize that is now widely grown by farmers for cattle fodder), for robinia as a fast-growing fuel, for straw plaiting as a way of providing an income for countrywomen. Why should Leghorn bonnets make Italy rich, when plaiting straw for the bonnets could equally well be done here in England?

He loved England passionately. It is one of his most endearing traits. In England, he wrote, you could find grass and

turnips, mutton, beef and cheese 'in greater abundance and
of better quality than they are given to any other country in
the world'.¹ His radical views put him always on the side of
the people who actually had to do the work on the land he
rode through, not the people who owned it. Going from the
Wen (as he called London) into Surrey, he passed through the
immense estate near Horsham then owned by Lord Erskine.
'A most villainous tract,' he wrote on 26 July 1823. 'After
quitting it, you enter a *forest*; but a most miserable one; and
this is followed by a large common, *now enclosed*, cut up, disfig-
ured, spoiled, and the labourers all driven from its skirts. I
have seldom travelled over eight miles so well calculated to fill
the mind with painful reflections.'²

Arthur Young would never have written that. Nor William
Marshall. All three men had the state of English agriculture
as the focus of their writing. But Young and Marshall looked
forward. Cobbett looked back. Young and Marshall saw enclosure as an inevitable result of the need to produce more food
for an increasing population. Cobbett railed wildly against the
enclosures, the end of the commoners' right to cut turf and
fuel from the waste lands and to keep cows and pigs, sheep and
geese on the commons. He wrote his *Cottage Economy* (1821)
for these people, showing how, with sufficient industry, rural
families could gain self-respect, become self-supporting and
independent. As with John Seymour, who wrote *The Complete
Book of Self-Sufficiency* in the 1970s, the time and labour self-
sufficiency demands were rather glossed over.

Although Cobbett had set up his own nursery at Kensington,
on the western edge of London, he loathed the creep of the
Wen into the country, particularly the arrival of the 'stock-
jobbers', pursuing wealth not for any decent social purpose
but for its own sake, making a living by producing money, not
corn or cattle, timber or sheep. He wanted to turn the clock
back, to restore the undisturbed scenes of his childhood in

the vales around Farnham, Surrey, where he had been born in 1763. Unlike the Chartists, who wanted a new moral order, he wanted the old order, the pre-industrial order, which he remembered (selectively no doubt) as a golden time. On 4 December 1821, at Elverton Farm, near Faversham in Kent, he writes fiercely of his conviction that the wens will 'moulder away', that the 'ridiculous' new houses covering the old common lands, 'these rubbishy, flimsy things, on this common, will first be deserted, then crumble down, then be swept away, and the cattle, sheep, pigs and geese will once more graze upon the common, which will again furnish heath, furze and turf for the labourers on the neighbouring lands.'[3]

It was because of this sympathy with the labourer (the *Political Register* had a circulation of *c*. 60,000, mostly among working men) that Cobbett always felt happiest in relatively sheltered, well-wooded country. He felt no connection with the high, open landscape of the Cotswolds, which he visited on the first of his rides. Going towards Cirencester in October 1821, he notices fields 'fenced with stone, laid together in walls without mortar or earth. All the houses and outhouses are made of it, and even covered with the thinnest of it, formed into tiles. The stiles in the fields are made of large flags of this stone, and the gaps in the hedges are stopped with them. – There is very little wood all along here. The labourers seem miserably poor.' He noted their 'wretched hovels', stuck upon bits of waste ground along the sides of the road. It seemed, he wrote, 'as if they had been swept off the fields by a hurricane, and had dropped and found shelter under the banks on the road side . . . Any thing quite so cheerless as this I do not recollect to have seen.' The stone landscape he considered 'quite abominable'. What did people here do for fuel?[4]

Cobbett's *Rural Rides* rarely took him so far from home as this. Most of his subsequent journeys lay through Sussex and Kent, Surrey and Hampshire. In Kent and Sussex, blessed with plenty of trees, he felt the labourer had at least a chance of a reasonable life. The woods

> furnish fuel, nice sweet fuel for the heating of ovens and for all other purposes; they afford material for the making of pretty pigsties, hurdles and dead fences of various sorts; they afford materials for making little cow sheds; for the sticking of pease and beans in the gardens; and for giving to everything a neat and substantial appearance. These gardens, and the look of the cottages, the little flower-gardens which you see everywhere, and the beautiful hedges of thorn and of privet; these are objects to delight the eyes, to gladden the heart.[5]

In the high chalk lands round Salisbury, where fuel had to be bought, he remembered the miserable sight of the poor taking turns to make a fire so that four or five kettles could be boiled on the one flame. 'What a winter life must those lead, whose turn it is not to make the fire.'

He had little appreciation of the wild, natural beauty that, at this time, was drawing crowds of tourists to the Lake District, to North Wales and to the vast, uninhabited tracts of the Highlands. He had lived in America and Canada and France, but the world of the *Rides* is bounded, to a large extent, by the soft southern counties of England. In this world, for him, beauty is entirely bound up with use. The kind of landscape he responds to manifests itself in Mr Sloper's farm at West Woody in Hampshire: 'large tracts of turnips; clean land; stubbles ploughed up early; ploughing with oxen; and a very large and singularly fine flock of sheep. Everything that you see, land, stock, implements, fences, buildings; all do credit to the owner; bespeak his sound judgment, his industry and care.'[6] Cobbett likes a landscape to be productive, shipshape.

Though towards the end of his life he represented Oldham in parliament, he had no knowledge of Blake's 'dark, satanic mills', no interest in the industrial cities of the north, and little understanding of the very different lives of those who worked in the factories and mills that defined them. 'Born among husbandmen, bred to husbandry,' he wrote in the *Political Register* in 1821, 'it is natural that I should have a strong partiality for country life, and that I should enter more into the feelings of labourers of husbandry than into those of other labourers.'[7] As a commentator, he had impeccable credentials: his father had farmed, in a small way; his grandfather had been an agricultural labourer. He looked the part too: dressed in woollen broadcloth, with an unwavering, slightly pugnacious gaze and, in the portrait painted about 1831, hand stuck confidently in the pocket of a waistcoat tightly buttoned over a swelling front. William Hazlitt epitomised him as a man who 'speaks and thinks plain, broad, downright English'.[8] Mary Russell Mitford, his neighbour at Botley, the Hampshire farm he bought in 1805, wrote that 'There was something of Dandie Dinmont about him, with his unfailing good humour and good spirits – his heartiness, his love of field sports, and his liking for a foray. He was a tall, stout man, fair and sunburnt, with a bright smile and an air compounded of the soldier and the farmer, to which his habit of wearing an eternal red waistcoat contributed not a little. He was, I think, the most athletic and vigorous person that I have ever known.'[9]

On the *Rides,* he travelled always in the same way, setting out on horseback from Kensington, usually with one of his sons in attendance. That seemed to be a purely practical arrangement. When the pair turned up at an inn for the night, the son took on all the business of getting their horses properly stabled and fed, while Cobbett, impressions still fresh in his mind, could immediately call for food and beer and get down on paper the detail of the day and the things he had seen. Even in town he kept country hours, rising at four and going to bed at eight. His object in the *Rides* was to hear 'what gentlemen, farmers, tradesmen, journeymen, labourers, women, girls, boys and all have to say; reasoning with some, laughing with others, and observing all that passes'.[10] He had a political agenda as well as an agricultural one. In the 1820s, when Cobbett was riding through the southern counties, English agriculture was in a depressed and distressing state. In his view, radical reform – universal manhood suffrage – was the only answer, and it was a message that he carried to the many political meetings he went to (usually uninvited) during the course of his rides. During the Napoleonic Wars, agriculture had been a hugely profitable business. Now it was in a slump. In the north, the coming of the Industrial Revolution manifested itself in giant factories and mills. In the south, the effects on the landscape were less pronounced, but farming techniques were changing. Agricultural labourers felt their livelihood threatened by inventions such as the new threshing machines that soon began to appear on the larger estates. And farmers who used, as a matter of course, to feed and house their work-people no longer did so. Why was it happening, he asked, and in the same breath answered his own question: 'Because they cannot keep them *upon so little* as they give them in wages.'[11] Cobbett, of course, deplored the changes, and his concern for the effect they had on agricultural workers – low wages, the enclosures, the Speenhamland system – never wavered. The Speenhamland system, launched in 1795, ostensibly to help the poorest labourers by making up their pay from the rates, had the effect, as Cobbett realised, of branding them as paupers, and robbed them of self-respect. As he saw on his travels, farmers had taken advantage of the system to keep agricultural wages impossibly low at a time when farm labourers made up the biggest proportion of the workforce.

To accomplish his plan of visiting farmers in their homes, noting the kind of work labourers were doing in the fields, he had to be either on foot or on horseback. If he'd travelled in a coach he estimated that he could have covered sixty-six miles in eight hours, but the coaches stuck to the main turnpike roads and would not get him into the 'real' country places. Besides, as he observed, 'To travel in stage coaches is to be hurried along by force, in a box, with an air-hole in it, and constantly exposed to broken limbs, the *danger* being much greater than that of shipboard, and the *noise* much more disagreeable, while the *company* is frequently not a great deal more to one's liking.'[12] Bundled along in a coach, he would not have been able to chat to the farmers in the market at Chertsey, or to the drovers bringing thousands of Welsh cattle (mostly heifers in calf) from Pembrokeshire and Cardiganshire to the fairs in Sussex. Nowhere was the news encouraging. At the Chertsey market, cows that in 1813 would have fetched £15 each did not sell even at £3.

Once he had a plan, he liked to stick to it, even if it meant riding at night to make up the miles he had not covered during the day. There were no maps of the byways he preferred to use, and the innkeepers, ostlers and postboys he and his son dealt with on their overnight stops knew only the turnpike roads. 'Those that travel on turnpike roads know nothing of England,' he wrote. From Hascomb to Thursley in Surrey, a journey he made on 23 October 1825, almost the whole way was across fields or commons or along narrow lanes. And though his stated aim was to 'ascertain the state of the crops', he was fully alive to the richness and beauty of the different landscapes that unfolded before him. Coming from Westerham in Kent, he had 'a most beautiful ride through the Weald . . . In one place I rode above a mile completely arched over by the boughs of the underwood, growing up in the banks of the lane. What an odd taste that man

must have who prefers a turnpike road to a lane like this.'[13] The
wonder is that these byways still exist. And walking through
them, we can still catch the same views that Cobbett wrote
about. Cobbett did very little walking. 'On foot', he wrote,
'the fatigue is too great, and you go too slowly.'

If his day had included the sight of a good field of 'radical
Swedes', such as William Palmer grew on his farm at Bollitree,
then he went to bed particularly happy. Too often though, he
found farmers obstinately broadcasting seed in the old way,
rather than adopting Cobbett's method of sowing in rows, four
foot apart. At Thursley, he wrote in his usual fiery manner, he
was looking at the best land in England for Swedish turnips.
The farmers there were indeed growing swedes, but in the
wrong way. If they had only followed Cobbett's advice, they
could be looking forward to crops double the size. Swedes,
turnips, barley, peas, apples, whatever the crop, Cobbett took
an interest in it. There was only one crop he did not like to see –
potatoes. Riding through Hertfordshire and Buckinghamshire
in 1822, he rejoiced in the fact that he had scarcely seen three
acres of them in the whole stretch of country from St Albans
to Chesham. He hated the potato because he thought that,
under the Speenhamland system, it was being used to pull even
lower the living standards of the English labourer. It was an
essential element of the cheaper diet advocated by those who
were urging vicious amendments to the Poor Laws. Cobbett
fought a long battle against the amendments, but unsuccess-
fully. The Poor Law Amendment Act was passed in 1834, one
year before he died.

Writing on trees, all the complex threads of his rides, his
reason for making them, come together: their importance in
the views of the English landscape he loved so passionately;
their value as timber, for land ought if possible to be useful as
well as beautiful; and his compassion for the un-propertied

poor – his observation, frequently expressed in the *Rides*, that in wooded country the lot of the agricultural labourer was slightly less hard than it was elsewhere. Riding back to London from Dover on 3 September 1823, he notes the wretched condition of the labourers in the district:

> Invariably have I observed, that the richer the soil, and the more destitute of woods; that is to say, the more purely a corn country, the more miserable the labourers. The cause is this, the great, the big bull frog grasps all. In this beautiful island every inch of land is appropriated by the rich. No hedges, no ditches, no commons, no grassy lanes: a country divided into great farms; a few trees surround the great farm-house. All the rest is bare of trees; and the wretched labourer has not a stick of wood, and has no place for a pig or cow to graze, or even to lie down upon. The rabbit countries are the countries for labouring men. There the ground is not so valuable.[14]

How different, he never tires of pointing out, is the hilly country round Hurstbourne Tarrant in Hampshire, one of his favourite places. Here there are fine oak woods, underplanted with ash and hazel, providing all the materials necessary for hurdles and fences. The woods stretched along the tops and sides of the hills for miles, twisting and winding about the pastures lower down on the slopes. They plunged into the long, deep valleys where rooks built in the elms. The mass of the woodlands, the spacey void of the pastures, it was a combination of elements endlessly repeated through the landscapes of southern England. And he loved them, expressed his love of them, not in the language that Wordsworth, say, used in 'Tintern Abbey' (published in the 1798 edition of *Lyrical Ballads*), but with no less depth of emotion.

In his Sussex journal of 1822 he noted how much more of interest to the traveller was offered by the woodland counties, 'not so much on account of their masses of green leaves,' he wrote,

> as on account of the variety of sights and sound and inci-
> dents that they afford. Even in winter the coppices are
> beautiful to the eye, while they comfort the mind with the
> idea of shelter and warmth. In spring they change their
> hue from day to day during two whole months, which is
> about the time from the first appearance of the delicate
> leaves of the birch to the full expansion of those of the
> ash; and, even before the leaves come at all to intercept
> the view, what in the vegetable creation is so delightful to
> behold as the bed of coppice bespangled with primroses
> and bluebells?'[15]

He appreciated too, that those who originally cleared wood-land from the lower slopes for pasture had followed the good soil, without regard to the resulting shape of the fields they were creating, so the woodlands themselves had endless variety in their forms and outlines.

Of all trees, the ash, he reckoned, was the most useful and the hardiest of all British native trees. Along the southern coast, he pointed out how even the firs leaned away from the gales blowing in from the sea. But the ash did not. Wherever it was planted, it grew straight and true. Oaks could be shaved up by wind, but ash always 'stands upright as if in a warm woody dell. We have no tree that attains a greater height than the ash; and certainly none that equals it in beauty of leaf. It bears pruning better than any other tree. Its timber is one of the most useful; and as underwood and fire-wood it far exceeds all others of English growth.'[16] Cobbett reckoned that if Lord Hardwicke at Tittenhanger Hall in Hertfordshire had planted ash instead of elm along the approach to his house, he might get a hundred pounds' worth of fuel cut as trimmings from the trees every year. On this Hertfordshire journey in January 1822 he spent a great deal of time computing the probable value of ash plantations and laying out the many ways in which the wood could be used. Nevertheless there were limits. In this county, his eye was 'constantly offended' by the sight of trees that had been heavily pollarded. Even on the meanest, poorest lands of Hampshire and Sussex, he fumed, you'd never see such an ugly sight.

He was, though, intrigued and delighted by a way of treating the edges of cornfields in Hertfordshire and Bedfordshire, which he had not seen practised in any other county. The custom was to leave a border round the ploughed part of the fields where grass could grow for a hay crop. Cobbett was there in June, when the hay had been cut and gathered, so round every cornfield was a closely mown grass walk about ten foot wide, between the corn and the hedge. 'This is most beautiful!' he wrote, enraptured.

> The hedges are now full of the shepherd's rose, honey-suckles, and all sorts of wild flowers; so that you are upon a grass walk, with this most beautiful of all flower gardens and shrubberies on your one hand, and with the corn on the other. And thus you go from field to field (on foot or on horseback), the sort of corn, the sort of underwood and timber, the shape and size of the fields, the height of the hedge-rows, the height of the trees, all continually varying. Talk of *pleasure-grounds* indeed![17]

But even in this rapture, he could not miss the opportunity to point out that the practice resulted in profit as well as beauty. The ground close to the hedges would bear little corn, but grass grew there perfectly well.

Cobbett's *Rides* generally started in Kensington, where he lived, but returning to the city through the suburbs, he could rarely resist an outburst against the stock-jobbers, the 'tax eaters', who, even then, were moving out from the city to settle in the villages of Surrey and Berkshire. He particularly hated the area round Windsor Forest, '*spewy sands* and *gravel*', where the roads were smooth and level enough for the wretched jobs-worths to get up by coach to the Exchange 'without any danger to their worthless necks'. Sunninghill made him so apoplectic you wonder he could stay in the saddle: 'a spot', he raged, 'all made into "*grounds*" and gardens by *tax eaters*. The inhabitants of it have beggared twenty agricultural villages and hamlets.'

In terms of his blood pressure, Kent was no safer. At Upstreet, on the way to Canterbury, he notes the irony of a sign reading 'PARADISE PLACE *Spring guns and steel traps are set here*.' It could only be a stock-jobber's place, he concluded. 'The name is likely to have been selected by one of that crew; and, in the next place, whenever any of them go to the country, they look upon it that they are to begin a sort of warfare against everything around them.'[18] This is still true, particularly with regard to footpaths. And cockerels. And mud on village streets.

He wasn't a lyrical writer. Or mystical, in the sense that infuses for instance Samuel Palmer's Shoreham paintings (Palmer produced *The Valley Thick with Corn* in 1825), but there are times when the wondrous nature of the views opening up in front of him, their diversity, their origin, their intricacy, stay for a time the torrent of righteous anger that pours out in the *Rides*. It happened in August 1823, when he pondered the strange sight of the Devil's Jumps, three hills that rise suddenly out of the common near Churt in Surrey.

How had they been formed, he asked himself? Surely it could not have happened by chance? How could waters 'rolling about' have resulted in such bizarre formations? But to think of them having 'bubbled up' from beneath was equally extraordinary. And how did those stripes of loam get there, running down through the chalk? What created the lines of flint running parallel with each other horizontally along the hills? He mulled over the part that the clouds played in the landscape, 'coming and settling upon the hills, sinking down and creeping along, at last coming out again in springs, and those becoming rivers. Why, it is all equally wonderful.'[19]

Though he found much to admire in areas such as Kent and Norfolk (the Norfolk farmers particularly he found 'very neat and *trim* in all their farming concerns'), it was in Hampshire, the county of his birth, that he always felt happiest. He liked a landscape of high downs with woods on the sides of the hills. He liked looking down on farmhouses, sheltered by stands of tall trees. 'This is my taste,' he wrote, riding from Winchester to Burghclere, 'and here in the north of Hampshire, it has its full gratification.'[20] He liked watching the slow movement of the great flocks of sheep coming down from the high, unfenced pastures to the fields where they were folded for the night.

On 24 August 1826 he was back in Uphusband, near Hurstbourne Tarrant, a country of chalk and flint, dry top soil and hard roads, bare, high hills and deep dells pierced by canopies of ash and elm. By the evening, he was sitting at a south-facing window of the inn at Everley looking out over the garden to a big clump of tall sycamores and 'a most populous rookery, in which, of all things in the world, I delight'. The sun was setting; the rooks were skimming and curving over the tops of the trees. Under their branches, Cobbett could see a flock of several hundred sheep, 'nibbling their way in from the Down, and going to the fold'. Here was his Arcadia.

Samuel Palmer, *Evening*, engraved by Welby Sherman (1834)

CHAPTER 10

Of Rooks and Sheep

C OBBETT'S SONS, WILLIAM, John, James and Richard,
would have heard their father's voice too often and so
had probably stopped listening to him, but I should
like to have ridden alongside Cobbett. He fought the right
kind of battles. He was, like many countrymen, wonderfully
observant of his surroundings. I would share his appreciation
of a good field of cabbages, such as he saw at Colonel Joliffe's
farm at Mearstam. Early Yorks, thought Cobbett, and probably
weighing at least three pounds each; for cattle feed, unparalleled. They would be at their best in October, when the grass
was beginning to run out. I would have respected and admired
his ability to read the agricultural and pastoral landscape,
to analyse what each part of it might mean for those whose
livelihood it represented. Sheep sound, oaks and hazels very
fine, hurdles well made, he observed in the chalk lands round
Winchester.

Of course, he wasn't looking at the land with the geological, the archaeological, the geographer's underpinning that
W. G. Hoskins later brought to *The Making of the English
Landscape*. But he had an intimate and sympathetic appreciation
of the work necessary to bring a field of corn safely through
to harvest, of the careful process of raising fine beef cattle,
worked out over generations of husbandry. And when he got
into a rant, as he so frequently did, about Pitt, or plaiting,

or paper money, I would just let my mind drift out and away over the fields and woodlands, noting, as he constantly did, the particular comfort represented by the cottages and farmsteads drifting through the sheltered valleys. 'You feel a sort of satisfaction,' he wrote, 'when you are out upon the bleak hills yourself, at the thought of the shelter which is experienced in the dwellings in the vallies.'

And then, Cobbett's favourite scenes always include sheep and rooks, the two creatures more intimately associated than any other with the English landscape, its moods and seasons. I'm looking at rooks now, in February, hopping between the branches of the larch tree in the garden, snapping off twigs to carry across to the line of alders in the valley below where they nest every season. The ground is littered with twigs blown out from trees in the winter storms, but they never pick up dead twigs from the ground. Not pliable enough, I suppose, nor capable of lasting as a new, freshly gathered twig might. But it's a laborious enterprise, carried out mostly by the males, since once the collection of twigs begins to look anything like a nest, the female has to sit in it to prevent it being taken over by other gazumping rooks.

The valley, with grassy pastures rising up on either side, is full of the flight of birds. Often we hear the flight, the thwacking whistle of air passing over (through? under?) the ravens' wings, or the thrilling measured beat of geese or swans flying in a V-formation over the valley. That doesn't happen often, but when it does, I always run out to watch them. I wave, and long to be with them. You can hear the pheasants taking flight, too, but that's an irritating, clattering noise. By nature, they are ground birds. They'd much prefer to run along the ground and hide in a bush than take to the air. Sometimes, if they've been forced to take off from high ground, they'll go into a long, downhill glide which is good to watch, but to me they will always be interlopers. Awkward birds, over-dressed and far too pleased with themselves.

The swallows are brilliant flyers – fast, energetic, acrobatic. They have a lot to do in a short time. With us, they nest in a woodshed with a stable door. The top half of the door happened to be open when they were casting about the garden, wondering whether to stay. And having investigated the woodshed, they evidently decided it would do. I have to walk past the shed quite often, but am never prepared for the way the birds zoom out right in front of my face. How can they get up such speed in such a short time? Just occasionally one of them rests on the television aerial on top of the house chimney and twitters madly in a constant, high pitch. Swifts scream and fly all at the same time. Swallows aren't so piercing. But I rejoice, in a quiet way, when I see four swallows in the air together, because I assume that, against all the odds in our often appalling summers, they have successfully managed to raise their young.

The best birds to watch, though, are the rooks, particularly when they are harassing the buzzards. The rooks leave the alders in small, determined posses to attack the bigger birds. The buzzards slide sideways down the wind, not intimidated, but temporarily ceding the airspace, knowing they will be able to return. From our terrace, with the land dropping away steeply and plenty of sky ahead, it's like watching a film of the Battle of Britain. The rooks, of course, are the Spitfires, the buzzards the slower, less agile German bombers.

Less agile? I wonder whether that's quite right. The buzzards are elegant in the air, slowly working their way up through the thermals in big sweeping circles over the valley. They seem to spend an extraordinary amount of time in the air, compared with the other birds that live here, but they rarely flap their wings. A favourite perch is a big oak with a dead head in one of the hedges. One or other buzzard flaps away from that from time to time. Otherwise they wheel silently, wing tips curved up in an entirely distinctive way. When we first came to Dorset, they were relatively rare. Not now. Early summer in the valley is full of the complaining mew-mew of some young buzzard, forced to find his own food.

The rooks are my favourites, as they were Cobbett's. They are handsome, agile, full of courage, industrious, companionable. And constant. Because they nest in the alders below us, their activities are, for me on the terrace, almost at eye level. They seem to have a vocabulary bigger than any other bird around here. The caw-caw is the most common perhaps, but there are plenty of other expressions, like the quick, clipped chip-chip noise they make when they are winging back into the rookery at the end of the day. They are intensely social and the rookery in the valley has at least sixty nests. When they leave the alders, they fly fast and purposefully, but I don't understand their movements. Why, on a fine summer evening at a quarter past nine, will they suddenly rise up out of the trees and wheel round in the sky, hundreds of them, shouting at each other? A cacophony of rooks, not going anywhere, shaping and reshaping into fluid dark pools and streams against the sunset. And then descending back into the trees. During the night you rarely hear them, but they play a big part in the dawn chorus that, during the spring, starts with us at about quarter past four.

Rooks animate the landscape. Constable, the countryman, understood that, including a crowd of them over the trees in his oil painting of *TheValley Farm* (1835).The artist David Cox (1783–1869) has them too, partly, he explained, because of the coarse wrapping paper he often used to paint on. He 'put wings' on any specks and imperfections in the paper and made them 'fly away as birds'.¹ By nature they are birds of plough and pasture. In the uplands their cousins the ravens take over. G. K.Yeates, who wrote *The Life of the Rook* (1934), reckoned there were 350 nests in the rookery he studied at Stodmarsh, north-east of Canterbury in Kent.There, they favoured Scotch fir and elm.The elms, sadly, are no more, but when in the early 1970s they began to disappear from the English landscape, the rooks quickly adapted and started to use other trees, as they did after the great storm of 1987.

During autumn and winter all the rooks in our valley retreat to a winter roost in the ash and sycamore trees behind the house. By early morning they've already left to forage in the fields.They're not like crows.They don't eat carrion. Then, in the evening, small, scattered bands return to the roost, clatter about companionably, exchange caws.Writing to the Hon. Daines Barrington, the Revd Gilbert White (1720–1793) noted how 'curious and amusing' the manoeuvres of the rooks were in autumn:

> Just before dusk they return in long strings from the forag-
> ing of the day, and rendezvous by thousands over Selborne
> Down, where they wheel round in the air, and sport and dive
> in a playful manner, all the while exerting their voices, and
> making a loud cawing, which, being blended and softened by
> the distance that we at the village are below them, becomes
> a confused noise or chiding, or rather a pleasing murmur,
> very engaging to the imagination, and not unlike the cry of
> a pack of hounds in hollow echoing woods, or the rushing

of the wind in tall trees, or the tumbling of the tide upon a pebbly shore. When this ceremony is over, with the last gleam of day, they retire for the night to the deep beechen woods of Tisted and Ropley.[2]

With us, though they roost in autumn and winter behind the house, they pay regular visits to their rookery in the valley, flying and circling above it, 'making that noise which they always make in winter mornings', as Cobbett noted at Wansdyke, late in October 1821. It's at this time that they seem most quintessentially part of the English landscape: the trees often bared in silhouette against the sky, the rooks swirling and calling over the newly ploughed fields, little else moving.

By February, they spend more time in the rookery, sitting in the branches, all facing the same way, beaks into the prevailing wind. They come in on a glide, two or three together, wings bent back into smooth sickle shapes. Conversation between them starts early, before dawn. By March, they no longer use the roost at night and spend all their time in the rookery. This is their noisiest time, but what are they saying? Is it all about territory? Are these KEEP OFF warnings to other rooks coming too close to the nests? Some of the nests survive from year to year in the alders, lodged high up, the trees still leafless though hazed round with the pewterbronze of their catkins.

The rooks spend most of spring in the exhausting business of bringing up their young. But by May the young birds are already on the wing, swooping out in exploratory flights down the valley. Sometimes it seems as if a couple of older birds take a pack of the young on an orienteering exercise, showing the way back to the nest from the pastures on the top of the ridge to the south, from the stone barns over to the north, from the big pond to the west.

During summer, the rooks are at their loudest around dusk between nine and ten at night, when they return to the alders in the valley. Some fly over the house from the north, but most come from slightly east, where their best feeding grounds must be. They arrive in purposeful groups, sometimes up to twenty at a time, more rarely alone, curling in over the trees and making immediate landings. That is such a skill, given that the speed and direction of the wind is never the same two days running. There's a certain amount of cawing, but the dominant sound is a constant short burbling noise. Their arrival is exactly timed to just after sunset, so they must leave where they have been feeding as dusk begins to fall. The last birds come in soon after ten and the noise from the rookery subsides about half an hour or so after it began. As the rooks return, the bats come out.

The most thrilling time to watch them is the beginning of autumn. By then, they've left the nesting site and gone back into the trees behind the house. But just when you think they might be concentrating on feeding themselves up for winter, they indulge instead in wild, tumbling feats of flying. Was this what Constable saw when he included a wild cloud of them in the sky over his *Hampstead Heath with a Rainbow* (1836)? Here, in our valley, a huge band leaves the roost trees at the same time, with a noise like people clapping with their gloves on.

Suddenly a small group will tip over, spreading their wing feathers, swooping down on the wind to climb up and join in larger gangs, weaving higher and higher. The noise is loud, loud. Sometimes they are very high, whirling round and round and round and sometimes three or four break away from the rest and seem to compete with each other in twists and plummeting dives and last-minute recoveries. The way they fly at this season is completely different to the purposeful comings and goings of the rest of the year. They go much higher for a start, really high. It's dizzying what they do. There must be several hundred of them in the air at once, free-wheeling in the air space of the valley. Three zoom down parallel with the alders. The speed is wildly exhilarating, twist, turn, up, like a surfer catching a wave. When they are sliding, gliding like this, not flapping their wings, the rook's body makes a beautiful shape, the wings curved back into a sickle. Then a wing tip will go down and WAAAAY, the bird goes into a steep dive, so fast. Is it instinctive, the way that the rook just sorts out that wing, trims it, as one might trim a sail to make better use of the wind? But sailing is something we have to learn. Do the young birds also try things out and find out WAAAAAY, so that's what happens when I drop the wing tip? Sometimes I can see the sky between the flight feathers of their wings. How brilliant they are. And how surprising. No wonder Cobbett loved them.

Through the branches of the rookery in the alders, I can see the sheep grazing on our pastures the other side of the stream. This has always been sheep land. Too steep for anything else. More than any other creature, wild or domesticated, sheep have been responsible for shaping our landscape. As it happens, the field they are in just now is a Site of Nature Conservation Interest with 113 different kinds of plant making up the sward. Without the regular presence of sheep these pastures would quickly revert to scrub: blackthorn would creep in from the boundary hedges, brambles would seed themselves in impenetrable thickets, gorse would gallop over the hill, with bracken not far behind. That is what happens if nature is left to her own devices. The complexity of old pasture is maintained by sheep, endlessly nibbling. Moles help too, because on the fresh earth thrown up in their tunnelling the flowers of the pasture can shed their seed, get a head start on the grass that is a tough competitor. But it's an irony that our field should be labelled as it is because the field isn't actually natural. Like most land in England, it's managed. And the sheep are crucial to its survival.

Quietly, calmly, as the day moves into evening, the sheep move up the slope to the top field, keeping ahead of the long winter shadows that begin to creep up the lower parts of the pasture. Cobbett wrote of the sheep, in the evenings, coming down off the hills. And, in those contrasting trajectories, we see one of the many changes between the agricultural practices of his age and our own. In the sheep country he was so often moving through, such as the chalky hills round Hurstbourne Tarrant in Hampshire, or the downs of Wiltshire where flocks of sheep grazed on the high grassy slopes, the practice during autumn and winter was to bring them down at night, on to fields that in the spring would be sown with corn, or turnips or cabbages. The sheep, shut up in pens made from hazel hurdles, manured the ground, adding valuable fertilizer to the fields. In the report he wrote for the Board of Agriculture in 1794, Thomas Davis, steward to the Marquis of Bath at Longleat, explained how sheep were managed on the downs, the huge sheep-leazes that ran from Burghclere in Hampshire, where Cobbett often stayed with his friend William Budd, right the way across to beyond Avebury in Wiltshire.

In Wiltshire, he explained, the high grassy sheep runs were still held in common, each commoner having a right to pasture a flock of a certain size on the great, unfenced tracts like those shown in William Turner's wonderful sweeping view of the uplands round Stonehenge, complete with shepherd and dog as well as flock.[3] The common sheep down was available for the combined flocks during the whole of summer and autumn. The fields lower down could be used as commons until they were ploughed for wheat. The sheep stayed up on the down till the harvest was over, when their owners could use the low ground again. Until the onset of winter, the flocks were folded all together on the arable fields, but when they began to need hay, each commoner was obliged to find his own fold and his own hay, though a single shepherd was responsible for feeding and penning all the different flocks of sheep. By the time the ewes had lambed, the water meadows would be ready for them. Some of these were privately owned, some held in common.

When the water meadows were being flooded (a technique used to encourage strong, new flushes of grass), the sheep were penned on land that would later be sown with barley. When the barley was sown, they moved back up to the leazes on the down until the stubble fields were broken up by the plough. Around the middle of September, the rams were turned in among the ewes. The rams were provided at the joint expense of the commoners, who also, jointly, paid the shepherd. As grazing began to run out, the flocks were reduced, with wether lambs alongside the older ewes being sold off around Michaelmas. The system did not allow for making hay, which had to be carted in, expensively, from outside the district. In Uphusband, in October 1822, Cobbett noted that the village was 'a great thoroughfare for sheep and pigs, [being driven] from Wiltshire and Dorsetshire to Berkshire, Oxfordshire and away to the North and North East'.

Cobbett completely understood how critical sheep were to the landscape and economy of downland country. Of the Wiltshire downs in 1826 he wrote:

> *Sheep* is one of the great things here; and sheep, in a coun-
> try like this, must be kept in *flocks*, to be of any profit. The

sheep principally manure the land. This is only to be done by *folding*, and to fold you must have a *flock*. Every farm has its portion of down, arable, and meadow; and, in many places, the latter are watered meadows, which is a great resource where sheep are kept in flocks; because these meadows furnish grass for the suckling ewes early in spring; and indeed, because they always have food in them for sheep and cattle of all sorts.[4]

John Claridge, who in 1793 wrote the *General View* of Dorset for the Board of Agriculture, also stressed the central role that sheep played in the economy (and therefore the appearance) of this deeply rural part of England. Of the 775,000 acres of land in the county, by far the largest proportion (290,000 acres) was taken up with ewe leazes and downs. They provided the area's 'most striking feature', wrote Claridge in his Introduction. These 'open and unenclosed parts, covered by numerous flocks of sheep, scattered over the Downs . . . are in general of a delightful verdure and smoothness, affording a scene beautifully picturesque'.[5] The Board of Agriculture's agents rarely allowed themselves the luxury of a view.

Sheep undoubtedly provided the greatest agricultural resource in the county, wrote Claridge, estimating that there must be at least 800,000 of them, vastly outnumbering the population, which he put at around 89,000. There was of course a profit to be made on the fleece, and the carcass, but, like Thomas Davis, he reckoned the greatest advantage they bestowed was the quantity of ground they manured. As in Wiltshire, the sheep ran over the downs by day and at night were penned in folds on the tillage. Before sunrise in winter, and never later than six o'clock in summer, the shepherd released the flocks from their pens and took them back up to the high ground to graze.

The hurdles used for the pens were made entirely from hazel, which is why, in sheep country, you still see so many big old stands of this tree, no longer regularly coppiced, but still producing from its base each year fresh wands of strong, whippy growth. And gorgeous waterfalls of catkins. (If hazel were rarer, if it had been brought into this country from Siberia or the Rockies, gardeners would be mad for it. But it wasn't and they aren't.) Fifteen dozen hurdles would enclose 1,300 sheep on an acre of ground. The hurdles were moved every morning, so that each day a different acre of ground would receive its manure. In this system, the role of the shepherd was critical. A good one could expect a wage of six shillings a week (roughly £450 in today's money), a new greatcoat every year and breakfast on a Sunday. He himself was responsible for finding and feeding a sheepdog, which, even in this age, few sheep farmers can do without.

In great detail, Claridge describes the characteristics of the Dorset sheep, short in the leg, 'the horn round and bold'. The horns, curling round either side of the face, is what a stranger might most remember. But for our farming neighbours, who still keep herds of these sheep, the chief advantage of the breed is that they will lamb twice in eighteen months. So the fields round here often have lambs skipping about in September. Over on Portland, only twelve miles away, quite a different kind of sheep developed: smaller, bred for stony heathland, able to survive on much thinner pickings than the Dorset Horn or the Dorset Down.

This selective breeding had already been going on for centuries before Robert Bakewell (1725–1795) started his famous experiments in stock-breeding on his farm near Loughborough in Leicestershire. Using, it is thought – Bakewell was notoriously cagey about his methods – existing

strains of Lincolns and Ryelands, Bakewell produced the
Leicester, a small-boned, square-bodied animal, highly profitable for those who bred sheep primarily for meat. He had
plenty of publicity from both Arthur Young and William
Marshall, and by the 1770s he was making £3,000 a year
by hiring out rams. One year, his best stud ram, known as
Two Pounder, earned Bakewell 1,200 guineas. At Wynford
Eagle in Dorset, reported John Claridge, farmer Bridge had
been the first to introduce the Leicestershire breed into the
county, crossing them with the native Dorsets. Not everyone
was in favour. The meat would surely not be as good, and,
perhaps more to the point, if Mr Bridge's Leicester crosses
produced lambs in the same season that the Dorsets did, it
could open up trade in other parts of the country to supply
the London markets with early lamb – trade which, here-
tofore, the west country farmers had had pretty much to
themselves.

In the southern counties, Cobbett was mostly seeing
the fine, stocky Southdown sheep with wide foreheads and
woolly faces. In the east of the country, it would have been
the handsome black-faced Suffolks, whose rams have for
a long time been popular with farmers. But are they, too,
on the way out? One autumn, I watched three rams busy
among three flocks of sheep pastured in different parts of
Burghley Park, where for a while we rented a cottage. The
shepherd can tell very quickly how the rams are performing.
So can everyone else, because each of the rams is fitted with
a leather harness that fits round his shoulders and chest. In
a pouch at the front of each is a large block of wax crayon –
red, blue or green, depending on the flock. It is called the
ruddle (or reddle or raddle, depending on where you come
from). When a ram mounts a ewe, the ruddle leaves a large

tell-tale blotch on the ewe's back. It is blatantly obvious which ones are scoring.

The rams will have spent the summer months in exclusively male company. Little has been expected of them except a macho show of arrogance. But at tupping time, the heat is on with a vengeance. The ewes in the park were mostly North Country Mules, a hybrid cross that combines the milkiness and fecundity of Blue-faced Leicesters with the hardiness of Swaledale hill sheep. They are mottle-faced, bare-legged creatures, not the most alluring sheep on earth. The red and green rams did not seem to hold this against them. Each day the number of ewes with red or green on their backs increased impressively.

Not so the blues. Suspiciously few blotches were appearing among this particular flock. The blue ram was a Suffolk, with the black face and handsome profile of the breed. The effect is rather spoiled if you look at a Suffolk head-on. The ears are laughable, sticking out from his head at a very strange angle. Even so, this Suffolk was good at confrontational postures. But not, evidently, so good at the rest.

He got out of breath easily. That was one of his problems. He must have weighed at least 180 pounds. Like all Suffolks, he had a broad back and thick, tight fleece. He was dogged, but often seemed to be pursuing the wrong quarry. One morning he spent three-quarters of an hour heaving and puffing after a ewe whose mind could not have been further from copulation. She nibbled the grass. He nibbled her backside. She moved on. He trotted after her, head stretched out, mouth open, billows of steam issuing into the frosty morning air. He prepared for the great heave-ho. She moved on again. He crashed to the ground. It went on more times than could have been good for his morale.

Even when he did score, it seemed to be with the few ewes that he had already successfully tupped. I didn't blame him for this, of course. It might even be therapeutic, going some way to repairing his self-esteem. The ewes, his familiars, showed no sign of resenting their role as therapists. The shepherd took a dimmer view.

Shepherds these days do not look like the ones that John Claridge and Cobbett described. They have mobile phones tucked in the inside pockets of their waterproofs and they drive Toyota trucks in the fields, swerving and swooping round obstacles as they check on their charges. But they still tell you that there is no money in sheep.

The shepherd arranges the tupping depending on when he wants his ewes to lamb. The main aim is to turn the ewes and their new lambs out to coincide with the first flush of spring grass. But market forces sometimes rearrange the timetable, making it worthwhile to feed sheep inside instead. Early lambs command higher prices. Geography plays a part, too. The tougher the country, the later the lambing. Apart from Dorsets, which work on an entirely different cycle, shepherds aim for a lambing between the end of February and the middle of April. Gestation is around 150 days.

It is obviously to the ewes' advantage to have their lambs at a time when there is plenty to eat. Oestrus, the period when their sexual organs are switched on, is cunningly linked to day length. The hours are clocked through the retina of the eye.

At Burghley, I watched the shepherd bumping through the park one day, neat piles of new crayon blocks in all the primary colours stacked on the front seat of his red truck. Every two weeks the blocks in the rams' harnesses are changed, partly because they wear out (if the ram is in business), partly because switching each flock to a different colour makes it easier for the shepherd to predict when each ewe is likely to lamb.

By this time, the Suffolk ram was spending most of his days in a corner by the fence, gazing glumly at the athletic activity of the ram in the neighbouring flock. This was the red ram, a Texel with an ill-tempered, triangular face – white, with a crease along the brow, which made him look very disagreeable. Now thought of as a French interloper, the breed originally came from the Netherlands, and is noted for the leanness of its meat.

The shepherd, of course, had also noted the discrepancy in performance between the different rams. The English Suffolk, he agreed, was not keeping his end up. 'The Texels work harder,' he said. 'They have a better style.' What did he mean by style, I wanted to know. 'The Suffolk wastes a lot of energy going where he's not wanted,' he said. I said I'd noticed.

'The French rams do it the other way round,' he went on. 'They don't bother to pursue. They wait for the ewes to come to them. And they do.'

'Why?' I asked, but the reason was as much a mystery to him as it was to me.

'It's in the blood,' was all he said.

As well as renewing the colour blocks in the rams' harnesses, the shepherd aimed to swap the rams around – put the red ram in with the green flock, the green with the blue, and so on. We both found ourselves looking towards the same ram in the same corner of the park. 'It gives them a new incentive,' said the shepherd as he accelerated away at speed to the sound of Michael Jackson's 'Black or White' on the truck radio.

I hoped the Suffolk would get the message. If he didn't, there would be no more lazy summers in the pasture, shooting lines to fellow members of the rams' club. In this increasingly competitive world, looks are no longer enough. If you don't make it in the sack, you are dogmeat. For rams, autumn is a testing time.

Paul Nash, *The Wood on the Hill (Wittenham Clumps)* (1912)

CHAPTER 11

Common Land

THE SYSTEM OF rearing sheep using common land that Thomas Davis (among other commentators of the time) describes required a nice understanding among commoners of their rights and responsibilities. Its complexities could only hold in a society where everyone understood the unwritten rules and respected the undrawn boundaries. It was a system that needed (and cemented) continuity. The hated enclosures were less of an issue in the west country, affecting less than thirty of the 260 parishes. The Dorset dialect poet William Barnes (1801–1886) never mentioned them. Wessex had the Tolpuddle Martyrs who fought for the rights of agricultural workers, but it did not have a John Clare to lament the enclosures. It was the arable lands of the Midland counties that bore the brunt of the enclosure movement, though, paradoxically, some of the first Acts of Parliament proposing enclosure were brought by Dorset landowners, wanting to enclose land often with the purpose of managing it as water meadow.

The tithe map (1839) of our neighbouring parish, Powerstock, shows that common land still played an important part in the lives of the people who lived in the village. The biggest of the commons was Poor Wood (289 acres), described as 'rough pasture' where thirty-five people are listed as joint 'landowners' of the common and twenty-nine as 'occupiers', with the right to graze livestock. Yet the way these rights are listed in the document that accompanies the tithe map reinforces the notion that the system could only hold in a tightly knit, stable community. Of all who shared ownership of the common, only fourteen took up their right to occupy it. Did the other fifteen 'occupiers' feel as secure in their rights? The list is very precise in laying out who could do what: Ann Wallbridge, right to graze two and a half cows in Poor Wood; Charlotte Shepherd, right to graze three and a half cows in Poor Wood; Joseph Whittle, right to graze half a cow in Poor Wood. Half a cow? How does that make sense? But in 1839 everyone in Powerstock would have understood what that meant, and everyone would have noticed if Ann Wallbridge, Charlotte Shepherd or Joseph Whittle overstepped their allotted right. For the commoners of this village, the common was an important agricultural resource; it was the means whereby land was made available to people who owned little or nothing themselves, giving them at least the prospect of raising a pig for meat, or a cow to provide milk and cheese.

True commons have their roots in the medieval system of land tenure, when the lord of the manor, who owned all the land, bagged the best bits for his exclusive use and the poorer people, the commoners, secured specific rights on the rest. They could graze animals, gather wood, bracken and turf. If they were lucky they could catch fish. There were six specific rights of common, including estover, the right to take wood from a common (important if you were a hurdle maker, or needed to repair a pigsty), turbary, the right to cut turf for fuel, and pannage, the right to graze animals on beech mast and acorns. This right is still exerted in the New Forest (run under its own rules), where each season herds of pannaging pigs happily stampede through autumn picnics. But many commons have lost their old, economic purpose and gradually acquired new ones, more to do with access, recreation and the conservation of wildlife than the survival of poverty-stricken labourers.

Commons do not exist in Scotland, where they do things differently, but you will find them in all the counties of England and Wales. There are huge commons for instance in the heather-covered uplands of Dartmoor and in Cumbria. If you measure by area covered, the three northern regions of England, together with the south-west, account for 87 per cent of all common land. But in the south, there are ancient wooded commons such as Ashdean and Epping Forest. There are grassy commons such as at Port Meadow in Oxford, sandy commons in Surrey and Suffolk, where heathland was of low agricultural value. In the fat cat county of Northamptonshire there are only thirty-six commons, thirty-two of which are less than an acre. Land here was too good to leave unenclosed.

There have been battles for commons ever since commoners' rights were first granted. Much was lost in the wave of enclosures in the eighteenth century. A hundred years later, the Commons Preservation Society was founded in response to the wave of speculative building that boomed in the 1850s. It had some powerful people amongst its members: John Stuart Mill, Charles Dilke, the Duke of Westminster. The Society fought hard to retain the forest commons of Waltham, Hainault and Epping. They organised a public subscription to buy Kenwood, now part of Hampstead Heath. They engaged in a historic manoeuvre at Berkhamsted, where Lord Brownlow had fenced off 434 acres of the common and taken it into the park of his home, Ashridge House. The Society employed 120 navvies who travelled on a special train from Euston to Tring armed with chisels and crowbars. They arrived at 1.30 in the morning and by 6 a.m. had torn up all the fencing – two miles' worth of iron palings – while their supervisor, too drunk to board the train with his charges, slept off his hangover in London. More recent attempts to protect common land have been less stirring. Because of the grand muddle that commons were in after the last war, requisitioned, ploughed and dug for victory, a Royal Commission sat down in 1955 to debate the whole issue. They made three recommendations: all commons should be recorded, all should be open to the public and all should be properly managed.

With a great deal of clanking and heaving, the Commons Registration Act came into being in 1965. This required that county councils should set up registers of commons with details of their owners and those who had common rights over them. It seemed a good idea at the time, but in certain instances the act backfired. Instead of protecting commons, it was sometimes used as a way of getting rid of them. Before legislation, while there was still a general fogginess surrounding ownership and rights on common land, developing or 'improving' it was not an option: you could never be sure that some person would not emerge from the wood claiming rights of estover, pescary or pannage. Once the registers were finished (the law allowed only three years for the process, so many were left off), it was clearer who owned what. This meant that some more rapacious owners, who managed to persuade commoners to give up rights, could then set about deregistering 'their' commons, a process made possible by a loophole in the drafting.

But registration, with all its faults, was only the first step in a process that was supposed to include management of and access to common land throughout England and Wales. In 1986 the Countryside Commission brought together a large group of interested parties to work out ways of implementing the access and management proposals. The Common Land Forum's report suggested ways of damming the leaks in the 1965 Act, preventing further deregistration of common land. It also called upon the Secretary of State 'to appoint a day in which public access would be granted on all commons'.¹ It set out provisions for a model management scheme which would specify what could happen on a common: what could graze there, whether or not horses could be ridden over it. The scheme also allowed for possible restrictions on public access if necessary. Any such restriction would need the consent of the Secretary of State.

The report was a considerable achievement. Its signatories included the Country Landowners' Association, the National Farmers' Union, the Ramblers' Association, the Nature Conservancy Council and other lions and lambs that do not normally lie down in the same pen. But still nothing happened. No legislation. No model scheme. Some argued that the desire for universal access to commons and the desire to conserve wildlife on them were mutually opposed aims. The Ramblers' Association's commitment to a general right to roam on common land had all the political fervour of the suffragettes' right to vote. It is a fine principle, provided that inherent in it is the responsibility of how to roam. The Association organised a series of mass trespasses at forty different locations, including the commons of Thurlstone Moor in the Peak District, owned by the newly privatised company, Yorkshire Water.

These bullish confrontations did little to further the cause of the commons. Lost in the middle of the fighting was the hoped-for legislation, which needed to cover many issues other than access. But the government's promise 'to work towards better arrangements for common land management' moved one step further forward with the Commons Act 2006, which recognised commons as 'precious reserves for biodiversity and recreation', as 'a vital agricultural resource' and as 'a strong feature of the English landscape and culture'. In that order. So the 372,941 hectares of common land registered as 7,052 separate commons moved a little closer towards full legal protection. At least Brussels didn't have to get involved. Despite being measured now in hectares rather than acres, these scattered parcels of heath and scrub and wood and grazing land have no counterpart in Europe. They are unique to England and Wales.

The names are evocative – Sam Bell's Common, Poor's Wood, Free Heath, Goose Marsh – but the problem with commons (those in the country at least) is that they are not what we think they are. The title gives the impression that this land belongs to us all by right, that it is held in common. This is not so. All commons are owned by someone, somewhere. Many are privately owned. As the law stands, only people with commoners' rights have a legal right on commons. The rest of us are there by invitation. Or not, as the case may be.

For a long time, the problem was compounded by the difficulty of finding out where commons were, for not everything called a common *is* a common. Common land is not marked as such on Ordnance Survey maps. For a local map, you might have tried your local reference library, which would perhaps have referred you to the council planning department, which would send you to the map bank, which would send you back to the planning department, which then redirected you to the rights-of-way officer, who thought he remembered a map kept in the solicitor's office. At least that situation has changed. When you finally gaze at the maps, the shape of the commons, the raggedness, the randomness of these dots and strips and nibbled parcels of land is testimony to the remarkable and stubborn survival through the centuries of common land and the particular landscapes they encapsulate.

The 2006 Act was a response to the challenges and difficulties which had arisen since the 1965 Act. Many commons still did not have mechanisms in place to ensure that they were sustainably managed. Some commons had proved vulnerable to encroachment, illicit development or other forms of abuse. The Register of Commons, hastily pulled together in the sixties, had been shown to be out of date and unreliable and so did not provide the kind of solid foundation that was needed in order to plan a secure future for these scattered remnants of land. In the Memorandum presented to Parliament in February 2013, the Secretary of State for Environment, Food and Rural Affairs (DEFRA) gave his response to the 2006 response, acknowledging that no single management system would fit all commons. On the uplands, grazing practices continue in the old way. Hill flocks are hefted to their piece of land. Elsewhere, the legislators proposed commons councils – 'democratic structures' through which commoners, landowners and others with an interest in a particular common, could work together for the general good. 'Three proposals are presently being considered by DEFRA,' reported the Secretary of State, 'but none has yet been established.'[2]

Will they survive? Perhaps – some as dog runs, decorated with neatly tied plastic bags of dog excrement hung from the trees, some in the hands of Wildlife Trusts. Powerstock Common is now managed by the Dorset Wildlife Trust, and is very beautiful, especially when seen on an autumn morning from the outer ramparts of Eggardon, the Celtic hill fort that was an important centre before the Romans even came to Britain. Of course, it's not the same common that Ann Wallbridge and Charlotte Shepherd knew, when their cattle grazed here in 1839. It is managed with different priorities. Parts of it still need to be grazed, but the primary object of the grazing now is to maintain particular habitats, carefully coded by Natural England. There is woodland, some ancient, some semi-natural, pasture both unimproved and restored, the inevitable scrub, several ponds with newts and dragonflies, an old brick kiln, devil's bit scabious and dyers' greenweed in the open, grassy areas alongside the route of the old railway line that skirts the northern boundary of the common.

The line reminds us of the transience of human affairs, compared with the flowers, the trees, the insects, and the birds that have been pitched here on the common for millennia past. When we were barely emerging from our caves, that buzzard, cruising over the complex, interrelated landscape of

Powerstock Common, had already been for thousands of years not only a beautiful but also a supremely co-ordinated creature. We have come late on the scene and it is presumptuous of us to suppose that, as humans, we are necessarily better equipped to understand the plot.

Howard Phipps, *A Beech Shaded Hollow, Cranborne Chase* (1992)

CHAPTER 12

Landscape and Farmers

THE SURVEYS MADE of common land in England and Wales were attempts to understand the history and background of one particular type of landscape, and to map its existence and extent. Maps, in the sense that we understand them, as interpreters of our surroundings, began with Christopher Saxton and his *Atlas* (1574–9), which, published county by county, showed the main features of the place: rivers, hills and towns. He showed no roads, few as they were. John Speed's *Theatre of the Empire of Great Britaine* (1611–12) added roads, as well as little vignettes of the most important places – York, Lancaster, Cambridge. Maps fixed a kind of identity for the country, encapsulated particularly in the magnificent series of Ordnance Survey maps that started to appear from 1801 onwards. An OS map can tell us about hills and mountains, rivers and streams, roads, bridleways and footpaths, railways, towns and villages. Where contour lines close together in a gingery blur, we know the land there will be rising steeply, often from a valley below. County boundaries, parish boundaries are laid down and large scale maps even show us the shapes and sizes of fields. From a map, we can see where the woods are, conifer plantations, orchards. Church spires and towers (among the few navigational landmarks in the earliest maps) are still noted. History is threaded through Ordnance Survey maps with ancient monuments or the names and dates of battlegrounds. So, with these magnificent sheets in front of us, we can read a landscape in its physical sense. We can make a rough assumption about the environment we are likely to find there, and the balance that exists between town and country areas. An OS map is a miracle of clarity; a miracle, too, in the amount of information it can give us in a limited space.

But a map such as this cannot tell you what exactly is happening in any of the spaces that it carefully delineates. Those orchards – are they cider orchards, where ancient trees, pushed over by gales, still bear vast crops of pitted cider apples in autumn? Or are they damson trees, throwing their flowers into the uncertain embrace of an early spring? Damson orchards are still a defining feature of the Lyth Valley in what was once Westmorland, but you'll see them now in relatively few other places in Britain. These small particularities of our landscape, and the pace at which we were losing them, was what drove Sue Clifford and Angela King in 1982 to set up Common Ground. Most conservationists work at saving rare things: whales, wild orchids, certain butterflies, fifteenth-century wall paintings. But by the early 1980s it became increasingly obvious to King and Clifford that it was the ordinary things that were becoming rare.

The name, Common Ground, sounds solid enough. It suggests cooperative ventures, common sense, a parallel combination of the practical and the philosophical. You remember vague connections with parish maps, community orchards, apple days, but you can never quite put a finger on the connecting thread. The connecting thread is local distinctiveness. They instigated projects that reinforced local identity, making you more aware of how your own patch in Devon or Dorset or Wiltshire is different from someone else's patch in Cumberland or Northumberland. Common Ground showed what you could do to reinforce the differences, fight homogeneity. Local building styles and materials – cob and thatch, granite and slate – used to be one of the most powerful ways of saying, 'You are here.' People in country areas used what was to hand when they built barns and farms, cottages and sheepfolds. If you had plenty of mature trees, you used a great deal of timber in your buildings (as in Herefordshire). If you didn't have stone, you used mud (as in the cob buildings of Devon), or baked bricks from the surrounding clay (as in Hampshire and Northamptonshire). Riding through the Cotswolds, William Cobbett remarked on the fields 'fenced with stone, laid together in walls without mortar or earth', a kind of landscape (and stone) he had not seen before. But now you can get 'Cotswold' stone anywhere. And 'Welsh' slate. And 'Sussex' tiles. The spread of the monster supermarket into the fields that once surrounded country towns has done nothing, either, to reinforce a sense of local identity. If it is tithe barn, it must be Tesco. If it is sub-Italian, it is probably Waitrose. Whether it is actually Dorchester, Yeovil, Saxmundham or York is neither here nor there.

One of the first ideas that Clifford and King floated was the Parish Map project. This had little to do with the Ordnance Survey, more to do with what local communities felt was important in their patch. Maps have been painted, woven, collaged, photographed in Muchelney and Penkridge, Nassington and Redlynch. They contain field names, legends, elements of natural history, local landmarks, ponds, barns. The making was not an end in itself; the maps, publicly displayed in village halls, provide a reminder to local people, a benchmark by which change could be measured.

And then Common Ground began to commission artists such as Andy Goldsworthy and Peter Randall-Page to create works that celebrated particular patches of landscape. If you walk the Dorset coast path, for instance, you will find a Randall-

Page shell built into a dry-stone wall on the Weld estate near
Lulworth. On Portland is a more complex project, a land work
by sculptor John Maine, celebrating Portland's long tradition
of quarrying. Five stone terraces, whose shapes echo the strip
lynchets of the local landscape, now snake across the landslip
area where Chesil Bank comes to an end. Maine worked on
the project for about seven years. In Devon, you will find one
of Randall-Page's superb sculptures lying like a great seed on
an island in a stream; another, like the two halves of a brain,
split either side of a long avenue of beech trees; another like a
rock with a spring bubbling through it. The works are strong
and physical, each one drawing from, reflecting and reinforcing its particular surroundings.

But the concept of local distinctiveness is full of paradox.
How do you even start to define it, now that people are
endlessly on the move and the raison d'être of communities,
both rural and urban – mining villages, cotton towns –
disappears with the jobs? 'The things that have been can still
inform and enrich,' says Clifford firmly. 'Change can happen
in a positive way. The dance goes on and when new people
enter into it, it is revitalised, enhanced.' It is not always easy,
though, to protect and defend local distinctiveness. In the
lane that ran past our first house, a brick-built cottage near
Petworth in Sussex, two enormous and very beautiful slabs
of Sussex marble, jammed with fossils, led up to the churchyard on the opposite bank. The bank itself was quite rough,
but covered with primroses in spring. There were even a few
glow-worms. But one morning a bulldozer arrived to carry
out a road-widening scheme. At whose request, no one in the
village could ever find out. Now, of course, I'd get straight on
the phone to the council (or the local wildlife trust) and ask
that the work be stopped forthwith on account of the glow-
worms. But back then, in the early seventies, wildlife wasn't

such an effective card in the fight for particular landscapes, however small. I told the dozer man about the primroses, and the glow-worms. I showed him the fossils, millions of years old, embedded in the great slabs of stone. He climbed into his cab, switched on the engine and lifted the arm of the huge machine to smash it into the bank. And I went inside the house, opened the windows on to the lane and played Liszt's Piano Sonata in B Minor at full volume on the record player. A requiem? No. I honestly believed the beauty, the passion of the piece would stop the dozer in its tracks.

The difficulty of fighting to save anything of beauty in our landscape, even so small a thing as two slabs of Sussex marble, lies now in the bureaucracy to be overcome. The bureaucracy is there to protect and help us, we are told, but after a ream of phone calls, a stream of 'pursuant to your communication of the 5th inst' stuff, you begin to lose sight of your object. It is a complex jigsaw, our landscape, and attempts to find the most effective way of understanding and managing it neces-sarily change as priorities change. That is what has made the issue of common land so intractable.

Landscape as bureaucracy started, in a way, with the Domesday Book. It was of course not about landscape at all, but about possessions. Who owned what? Why? But, as you can 'read' an OS map, so you can read landscape into the Domesday Book. Huge flocks of sheep – 600 at Abbotsbury, 900 on Portland, 1,037 at Cranborne, 1,600 at Puddletown in Dorset in 1086 – suggest an open landscape of heath and down. Ploughs suggest good arable land, watermills a landscape cut through with fast-flowing streams. Six thousand mills (both watermills and windmills) were listed in the Domesday Book. Work on it began in 1085, when King William, who had come and seen and conquered, wanted to know more about his new possession. The Anglo-Saxon Chronicle records that in 1085, 'at Gloucester at midwinter . . . the King had deep speech with his counsellors . . . and sent men all over England to each shire . . . to find out . . . what or how much each landholder held . . . in land and livestock, and what it was worth . . . The returns were brought to him.'[1] The southern counties were the first to be surveyed: Kent, then Sussex, Surrey, Hampshire, Berkshire, Wiltshire and Dorset. The commissioners had a clear brief. In each county they were to set down the name of each place, who held it before 1066, and who held it after the great redistribution of land with which William rewarded his supporters. The extent of the land was to be noted, measured in hides (one hide equalled about 120 acres) as well as the number of ploughs, cattle, sheep, pigs and goats. How many villagers were there in each settlement? How many cottagers, slaves and freemen? Questions were asked about the extent of the woodland, meadow and pasture, mills and fishponds. The evidence collected in the great book came from county sheriffs, local barons, priests and reeves as well as six villagers appointed from each village. Our encounter with a reeve is most likely to come from Chaucer's *Canterbury Tales*, but in the eleventh century a reeve was a powerful local figure, a kind of chief magistrate in the area.

From all this information came the *Liber de Wintonia*, the Domesday Book's real name, issued at Winchester in 1086, an immensely detailed roll call of rural England:

> Hugh holds Powerstock from Roger. Aelmer held it before 1066. It paid tax for 6 hides. Land for 6 ploughs . . . 5 villagers and 9 smallholders with two and a half ploughs and 3 hides . . . 2 mills which pay 3s; meadow, 13 acres; pasture, 15 furlongs in length and 2 furlongs wide; woodland 11 furlongs long and two and a half furlongs wide. 2 cobs; 4 cattle; 13 pigs; 158 sheep; 16 goats . . .[2]

The process of reading the landscape has continued to the present day, each report reflecting the prevailing concerns of the age. The Countryside Survey published in the nineties by the Department of the Environment was hailed at the time as the most comprehensive audit ever undertaken of the British countryside, a modern Domesday, though heavy on a word – Environment – that William and his counsellors would never have used. Based on a combination of satellite mapping and detailed field surveys, the document itemised the resources of the British countryside at the beginning of the 1990s: so much arable (34 per cent), so much pasture (29 per cent), so much marginal land (16 per cent), so much upland and moor (21 per cent). The survey team measured hedges, which were then still disappearing at an alarming rate, counted plant species on 11,500 vegetation plots and monitored 360 water courses. A previous audit, not so comprehensive, had been carried out in 1984 and the two reports, compared side by side, throw up some interesting indicators of the changing nature of the landscape in Britain. Broad-leaved woodland had increased slightly in the intervening years. But built-up areas had grown by 4 per cent, always at the expense of good agricultural land. The amount of arable land lying idle had more than doubled, an all too obvious sign then, as one travelled round the countryside, that the Government's set-aside scheme, introduced in 1988, had been enthusiastically taken up by farmers. This was not surprising given the level of compensation. On a decent arable farm, you could knock up a £15,000 cheque quite quickly.

The most depressing aspect of the report concerned changes in vegetation. Almost everywhere, plant colonies were less complex, botanical diversity reduced. Lowland, woodland, grassland were all affected, but for different reasons. In arable landscapes, the usual scapegoats – herbicides and fertilisers – were cited as agents of degradation. In the uplands, changes in grazing regimes were said to have affected the fragile mosaic of grass, heather and whin. But in order to make a living, hard-pressed hill farmers had to run an increasing number of sheep on the hills. If we paid a realistic price for meat (and milk) they would not have to. In the nineties survey, the richest habitats were shown to be the linear features in the landscape: hedges, verges, the banks of streams. The wider the verge, the more useful and diverse a habitat it provided. Meadow plants find an alternative home here. Their seed provides food for small animals. Nettles, cleavers, false oat-grass, blackberry and hogweed dominate verges in farmed land, a cruder landscape than the one that so delighted Cobbett riding through Hertfordshire in June 1822. In the uplands, soft rush, common sorrel, the hard fern, heath bedstraw and heather were the most common plants. Increasingly, in the mania for road widening, verges have been replaced by tarmac.

In its particulars, the Countryside Survey was a remarkable document. It provided immensely detailed information on land cover in Britain, on landscape features and habitats. It told what was happening in the countryside. But, crucially, it did not say why. Nor did it attempt to assess the significance of the changes in habitat for animals and birds. Or for us. Extrapolation was not part of the original brief. It was, however, immediately obvious that the findings of the survey would only be of value when they were integrated in a much larger scenario, one which involved the way that people lived and worked in the countryside. Habitats do not self-destruct. Changes in land use and the gradual degradation of the environment result from the things that are going on in it, and the value that is placed upon our landscape – its beauty and, critically, its capacity to sustain us.

In the nineties, the government had embarked on a road programme costing £23 billion, a process that continues unabated. The unseen, uncounted costs of our reliance on road transport are monitored in the Countryside Survey: roads, which in 1978 covered 3,300 square kilometres of the country, had, by 1984, gobbled up 4,500 square kilometres and the figure is still rising. In only six years, the amount of building in the countryside had increased by 4 per cent, another 800 square kilometres lost to tarmac and concrete. As we know to our cost, a huge increase in hard, impermeable surfaces affects the way that water is soaked up by the land. There is less sponge than there used to be, as was miserably obvious in the terrible floods in the winter of 2013–14.

And then, of course, there are the farmers. The Countryside Survey, commissioned by the Department of the Environment, was mapping changes that had to a great extent been brought about by an entirely different ministry, the now defunct Ministry of Agriculture, Fisheries and Food. The survey indicated that just over a third of Britain was arable land, concentrated in the Midlands and the eastern counties of England. Just under a third was pasture, grassland that was often as intensively managed as a ploughed field. Farming has a greater effect on the landscape and environment than any other activity, and it seemed sensible then that MAFF and the Department of the Environment should merge into a single body that could take a holistic view of what was happening out there between the houses, the roads and the out-of-town shopping malls. Unfortunately, farmers seem to have been vilified in the process. And our landscape, with its subtle, various, engaging, mesmerising beauties, has been reduced to a series of 'environments', each with its list of inhabitants. It was always going to be a shotgun wedding, with important adjustments to be made on either side. MAFF had to jettison its bullish, land-only-as-maximised-asset mentality. The environmentalists had to come to terms with the fact that the countryside is not one vast nature reserve, that people have to live and work in it. Farmers should be the conservationists' most valuable allies in creating the countryside that we all want to see: diverse, prolific, sustainable. But for this to come about, each needs to know more about the other's business. There have been occasional forays from one territory into the other – Environmentally Sensitive Areas, the Countryside Stewardship Scheme, Sites of Special Scientific Interest – but this piecemeal approach, combined with a pathetically low level of funding for the countryside in general, is not the right way to manage a resource as massive and as important as Britain's landscape.

The Countryside Survey of the nineties posed some interesting questions. What, it asked, was likely to be the long-term effect of the enormous increase in maize grown in the country – up three-fold, by 1994, from the acreage grown in 1984? Maize is harvested late, often in muddy conditions, with plenty of topsoil travelling on tractor tyres away from the fields and ultimately into ditches and drains. The fields lie bare over winter, and are not sown until late in the following year. How important are fields of barley as habitats? We may soon find out, as barley plummeted as a crop in the six years leading up to 1990. Human allergies to oilseed rape have been widely reported since it first blazed its noisy trail over the fields of Northamptonshire and Lincolnshire. What other, as yet unseen, effects is it having, particularly on insect populations in the areas where it is widely grown? Bee-keepers quickly found that the honey gathered primarily from rape behaved differently in that it crystallised (became solid) much more quickly than other honey.

For a short while rape was pushed out by linseed, the yellow fields replaced by blue. Farmers have to be businessmen and the level of support for rape was overtaken by that for linseed. But the problems of harvesting the crop, the way it blunted cutters, the way the threads of the stems tangled in the harvesters, put farmers off linseed. Then, in a strongly promoted burst of support for biofuels, farmers started growing elephant grass under contract to middlemen who reaped the real benefits. But it, too, was difficult to harvest and the power stations, after various attempts to use the stuff, often reverted to coal. And perhaps someone, somewhere, began to question the actual environmental benefits of carting bulky elephant grass 600 miles to the nearest electricity generating station, where, as it was burned, it produced even more carbon dioxide than coal. Renewable, yes, but toxic. As for the more recent march of the wind farms, listen to Owen Paterson, former Secretary of State for Environment, Food and Rural Affairs: 'This paltry supply of onshore wind . . . has devastated landscapes, blighted views, divided communities, killed eagles.'[3] New access tracks bite deep into previously undisturbed peat land and the production of carbon-intensive cement has been hugely increased because of the vast underground concrete platforms on which the wind turbines sit.

Those without land are always very quick to tell those with land what they ought to be doing with it. When he was launching the Countryside Survey, the then Environment Secretary, John Gummer, pointed out that the UK had pressed for environmental considerations to be integrated into the EU's Common Agricultural Policy (CAP), and had played a leading role in getting the European Community to include measures to encourage environmentally friendly farming in the CAP. Farmers recognise that the way they run their farms will be increasingly influenced by its effect on the wider environment, but theirs is a price-driven business. They produce what the government (or Brussels) pays them to produce. It can be pigs. It can be poppies.

For a while, opium poppies (*Papaver somniferum*) became a lucrative crop for British farmers. I first saw them a couple of years ago, shimmering in a field alongside the A35. It was the colour that caught my eye – too mauve for flax, too delicate for field beans. I swerved into a lay-by and trekked back to the field gate. Yes. Definitely poppies. Then I began to see great spreads of them, particularly around Oxfordshire, Northamptonshire and Lincolnshire, where the good, light arable land suits their needs. Poppy growing, I discovered, started on a commercial scale in this country because of a world-wide shortage of morphine. The seedpods of opium poppies are full of a milky latex which dries to an amber-coloured resin, rich in codeine, morphine, narceine, narcotine, papaverine and thebaine, all of significant use to medicine makers.

All the crops in Britain are grown under licence for a pharmaceuticals company. The company tells the Home Office where the crops are and how many acres have been licensed. The Home Office writes to the various farmers, confirming the arrangement and inviting them to let the local police know what they are doing. I haven't yet been joined by Plod on any of the occasions I've stopped to admire the poppy fields. Just as well, perhaps. It might not be easy to explain why I'm taking such an interest in them.

The advantage for the grower is that he doesn't have the bother of harvesting the crop. An Oxfordshire farmer pointed out that he has simply to prepare the land, drill the seed and watch the poppies grow. The pharmaceutical company with whom he has agreed the contract take care of the gathering and the processing. So it's not surprising that opium poppies were cultivated on at least 8,000 acres of arable land in Britain.

That's nothing though, compared to Tasmania, which has had as much as 20,000 hectares under production. It is the world's largest provider of opium poppies for the pharmaceutical industry. Inevitably, a story went around about Tasmanian wallabies getting high on the crop. They'd have to be hard-pushed to try it – it's very bitter – but perhaps equivalent myths will be forged over here: stoned rabbits, hallucinating deer, glassy-eyed sheep.

I was brought up among farmers, so it's perhaps not surprising that I don't share the view that they are ogres of the landscape, eating hedgerows for breakfast, spewing out nitrates for lunch and supping on a heady pudding of minced ramblers, seasoned with a sprinkling of conservationists. If only nature was allowed to take its course, people say. Freed from the grasp of the wicked agriculturists, how much more beautiful the landscape would be. We could picnic amongst carpets of cowslips and wild orchids. Clouds of butterflies would fill the summer pastures and the hedgerows would be alive with the sound of birdsong.

It is a fallacy that our landscape is an entirely natural phenomenon. Nature provided the raw material, the under-pinning, the geology of the countryside. The climate controls the way that the raw material can be handled, but the views that we croon over and write about, with too many adjectives, have very often been shaped by farmers. The process has been going on so long that, even as far back as Domesday, only 20 per cent of the country was covered in wild wood. It did not look as it does today, but nor was it natural. The landscape we know – the hedges, the fields, the mixture of pasture and plough – has been claimed, lost, reclaimed by agricultural activities, work which for centuries occupied the vast proportion of people living in England. Hedges, now so fiercely defended, were once equally fiercely opposed. In many areas, they are the result of one hundred years' worth of Acts of Enclosure that, between 1750 and 1850, allowed landowners to change the face of 4.5 million acres of open field. Almost overnight, in something like 3,000 parishes, a new landscape of hawthorn hedge and straight roads was imposed on the previous complicated pattern of open arable strips wound round by meandering cart tracks.

Ridge and furrow, now equally jealously guarded, was the prevailing feature of the landscape before the enclosures. It came about because of the kind of plough and the method of ploughing that farmers used then. It tipped the soil towards the centre of each strip, forming a high ridge. Like the hedge, it is a construct, a by-product of farming practice, not a natural phenomenon. What the landscape looked like before the first hunter-gatherer said, 'Blow this for a game of soldiers,' and stuck an ear of emmer in the ground instead, no one will ever know. Wordsworth tried to imagine it in his *Guide Through the District of the Lakes*: 'The primeval woods shedding and renewing their leaves with no human eye to notice, or human heart to regret or welcome the change.'[4]

The landscape we now see from the windows of a train, a car or walking down a country lane, will include a large proportion of land that in one way or another is managed. The changes in it will have been brought about by market forces, political manipulation, rarely by philanthropy. And, left entirely to its own devices, this land would not necessarily become more beautiful. Within fifteen years, pasture can become impenetrable scrub, overtaken by bramble, dock, Japanese knotweed, all the bully boys, swarming through the ditches and along the verges. There would not be poppies: the poppy is a flower of arable land, succeeding only where earth has been freshly turned over.

The real power to determine the face of the countryside still rests to a great extent with farmers, who for decades after the last world war were encouraged by successive governments to wring the last pint of milk, the last ounce of corn from their land. Farmers got extremely good at the job, took pride in running well-organised, productive farms. Then they had a new role thrust upon them: the farmer as conservator, rather than producer. Instead of being paid to bulldoze hedges, they got grants to maintain them. That was a radical change of gear, but with some grinding in the gearbox, they are getting there, because they are being paid to do so. Ardent conservationists might argue that the best solution would be for them to hold more land and the farmers less. The danger with this approach is that we slide even further down the road of country as theme park. 'Welcome to the Wessex experience. Please park prettily. While we have made every effort to minimise the presence of mud and ordure, we must warn visitors that overshoes (hire charge £6) may be necessary . . .'

No. This is not the way. There is already a danger that conservation bodies consider the needs of visitors more important than anything else: boardwalks, handrails, notice boards, mud-free car parks, all reinforcing the insidious notion that landscapes should be adapted to suit the visitor, rather than the other way round. Real landscapes, with all their inconvenience, must prevail against the tide that threatens to engulf us in a deodorised, sanitised masquerade of the real thing. It is unfashionable to champion farmers as stewards of the landscape, but that is where my vote lies. The survival of the views that each season draw millions of visitors into the Lake District depend to a great extent on sheep.

Samuel Palmer, *Early Morning* (1825)

CHAPTER 13

Dressing the Skeleton

FROM OUR TOP field we can see eight Celtic hill forts. In a landscape of unparalleled beauty, they are the dominant features, rising from fields and woods in a series of steep ramparts and ditches: bare Eggardon behind us, Lewesdon and Pilsdon out to the west, their lower slopes now wooded with beech and sycamore. On the characteristic grassy plateaux on top of these hill forts the first farmers quartered their animals, planted their crops. Our landscape in Britain is talked of now in terms of 'habitat', 'environment', 'wildlife', but, leaving aside the wild places of the mountains, our landscape is not, in the main, a natural phenomenon. Working at Frocester Court Farm, near Stroud in Gloucestershire, archaeologists uncovered evidence of boundary ditches dug around 1500 BC, sunken trackways and an Iron Age farm, well established by 200 BC with granaries, fenced pens for stock and a vegetable garden. Here, as on many other sites, is evidence that farming has been shaping the land for at least 2,000 years.

In *The Making of the English Landscape* (there are few books that can truly be described as seminal, but this is one of them) W. G. Hoskins traced the long slow process by which the geological skeleton of England, in itself remarkably diverse, was gradually dressed by farmers in clothes of ever increasing complexity and finesse. The one followed the other, of course. It is not caprice that brought the plough so intensively to the

Midland counties, with a consequent drive towards enclosure and loss of common land. It was the lack of problematic
heights, a gently undulating landscape underpinned by deep,
nutritious loam. And the need for people to eat, an imperative
rather forgotten in the modern age, when few people think it
strange to be eating beans flown in from Kenya or lamb that
has travelled halfway round the world from New Zealand.

Twenty generations of Anglo-Saxon farmers had worked
on the land before William and his conquering armies
arrived in England. Conquest meant a change of landlords,
but the farming had still to go on. Nearly every village on the
current map of England (with the exception of those in some
industrial areas) already existed by the eleventh century and
is included in the Domesday Book. The language and landmarks of those people live on in the place names that we
still use. They chart the topography of a landscape, its rivers,
streams, springs, lakes and ponds. Place names marked
moors, marshes and flood plains. They fixed river cross-
ings: 'ford' is one of the commonest topographical terms in
English place names, as at Bradford and Dartford, Guildford
and Oxford, Stratford and Watford. They indicated the existence of roads and tracks, hills and valleys, woods and forests,
plough and pasture.[1]

In the medieval period only six counties – Norfolk, Suffolk,
Essex, Lincolnshire, Devon and Somerset – had more than
50,000 people in them. But even then farmers were gradually
changing the way the landscape looked, pushing small fields,
barely an acre each, up on to the wastes of Dartmoor and
Exmoor, cutting down trees. On clay this was most likely to
have been oak and ash. Beech favoured limestone and chalk,
birch the more acid soil of the high ground. On the lowlands
elm, maple and lime were the most common natives. Sycamore,
now so widespread in country areas, the tree more than any

other you see planted to shelter solitary farmhouses on the windswept slopes of Cumberland or Northumberland, was unknown in England until the end of the sixteenth century. In the three most heavily populated counties – Norfolk (95,000), Lincolnshire (90,000), Suffolk (70,000) – one village in three had a watermill. Flat lands, these were. Good for corn. From the end of the twelfth century onwards new and important landmarks – windmills, church steeples – began to appear in the landscape, the steeples following the band of fine building stone that stretched across the country from Lincoln to the north coast of Somerset.

Ten generations of labourers in the years between the Norman Conquest and the Black Death dug ditches to drain marshland and moor to produce food for a population that by the middle of the fourteenth century had grown to about 4 million in England. In doing so, they created the kind of land-scapes that we hold to be so deeply characteristic of particular areas of the country: rich pasture bounded by a slow-running stream, pollarded willows standing on fat, hollowed trunks along its banks. Willow was as useful as hazel in producing hurdles and essential to make the baskets needed to carry butter, cheese and eggs to market.

The Great Plague reduced the population of England so drastically that for a time there was no longer any need to win fresh farming land from woodland, moor and marsh. In the more prosperous Midlands and in East Anglia, whole villages were deserted and sheep outnumbered people by at least three to one. 'The population of this island', commented an Italian, visiting England in about 1500, 'does not appear to me to bear any proportion to her fertility and riches.'[2] The 200 years that followed, from 1570 to 1770, represented, in W. G. Hoskins' opinion, a Golden Age for the English land-scape, before the Industrial Revolution, with its canals and factories and railways, gave this country a set of clothes unlike anything it had ever worn before.

Gregory King, who worked as secretary to the Commission of Public Accounts, estimated that in 1696, when he set down his *Observations and Conclusions upon the State and Condition of England*, at least half the land in England and Wales was under cultivation either as arable or as pasture or meadow. His chief aim was to assess population and wealth, but because wealth and land were so intimately connected we learn a great deal about the way land was farmed from the tables he drew up. Agriculture was the chief occupation of 150,000 farming families, on whom were dependent the 364,000 families of 'labouring people and out servants'. The farmers earned an average of £44 a year (£123,000 in today's terms), much the same as a shopkeeper; the labourer's wage was about a third of that, roughly equal to a soldier's pay. King showed that pasture and meadow land at 8/8d an acre (roughly £1,214 today) was more valuable than arable, at 5/6d an acre (£770). The 3 million acres of woodland and coppice scattered through the landscape, much more valued then than it is now, commanded 5s (£700) an acre, parks and commons 3/8d (£513), and the 10 million acres of heath, moor and mountain not much more than a shilling an acre (£140), for sheep keep.[3]

Since the early years of Henry VIII's reign, parliament had generally opposed moves by private landowners to enclose open fields. The earliest petition to be granted was one brought forward in 1604 to enclose land at Radipole, near Weymouth in Dorset. But from 1660, under Charles II and his successors, that changed, and even before the parliamentary enclosures in the early nineteenth century, half of Northamptonshire had already been hemmed into a straight-edged landscape of fields enclosed by thorn hedges. Riding through Norfolk in 1787, William Marshall noted the enclosures 'in general small, and the hedges high and full of trees. This has a singular effect in travelling through the country: the eye seems ever on the verge of a forest, which is, as it were by enchantment, continually changing into inclosures and hedgerows.'⁴ Marshall's comment about the hedgerows being high and full of trees suggests enclosures made decades previously, and it seems possible that even as early as 1700 perhaps half of the 9 million acres of arable land (Gregory King's estimate) was already enclosed with the view of increasing profits for its owners.

By 1750, the end of Hoskins' Golden Age, the momentum to enclose was unstoppable, particularly in the midland counties of Northamptonshire, Rutland, Huntingdonshire and Bedfordshire. Gone were the maps that the parishioners in those places had carried for so long in their heads, the maps built up from familiar trees, stiles, grassy headlands. Gone was their exact knowledge of whose labour had brought into productive cropping each particular strip of the old open-field system. Between 1761 and 1844 Parliament dealt with 2,500 acts to enclose roughly 4 million acres of land. After the General Enclosure Act of 1845, another 200,000 acres of open fields disappeared. As costs escalated in the war with France, more marginal land was brought into production and more than 2 million acres of heath, moor and common land was converted to ploughland and pasture.

At Helpston Heath in Northamptonshire, John Clare, born in 1793, was a witness to this savage process. As a boy he had watched over sheep and geese on this common; now the familiar landscape was being forced into a new mode. 'Took a walk in the fields,' he wrote in his journal on Wednesday 29 September 1824.

> Saw an old wood stile taken away from a favourite spot which it had occupied all my life the posts were overgrown with

Ivy & it seemed so akin to nature & the spot where it stood
as tho it had taken it on lease for an undisturbed existence it
hurt me to see it was gone for my affections claims a friend-
ship with such things but nothing is lasting in this world.[5]

The hawthorn hedges would most likely have been struck
from cuttings, and planted out as whips, not much more
than a foot high. Then, after twenty years or so, agricultural
labourers would have had to master a new technique, cutting
and laying the hedges to thicken them up and make them
more stock-proof. In 1790, the sharp-eyed William Marshall
described the procedure in his *Rural Economy of the Midland
Counties*; it was the first time he had seen such work going
on. The upheaval surrounding the planting of the hedges at
the turn of the eighteenth century was matched only by the
outcry against their removal in the 1960s and 1970s. For agriculturists, the reasoning both for planting and for removal was
the same: greater efficiency. The inevitable consequence of the
enclosures was that more and more land was consolidated in
the hands of fewer and fewer people. But in the rural areas
of England, unaffected by the even more cataclysmic changes
brought about by the Industrial Revolution, the landscape
created by the enclosures is, in the widest sense, the landscape
we look at today. The fields carefully numbered and marked
out, for instance, in the tithe maps made around 1840 for the
parishes of Netherbury, Powerstock and North Poorton in
West Dorset are pretty much the same size and shape now as
they were then. In the emerging industrial areas of the north,
it was very different.

For a brief moment, some commentators found the new
factories – John and Thomas Lombe's silk mill at Derby
(1718–22), Matthew Boulton's Soho Manufactory in
Birmingham (1765), Josiah Wedgwood's Etruria pottery in

Stoke-on-Trent (1769), Richard Arkwright's mill in Cromford, Derbyshire (1771) – as exciting as the natural phenomena of craggy mountains, wild waterfalls and thrilling precipices. 'The noise of the forges, mills etc. with all their vast machinery, the flames bursting from the furnaces with the burning of the coal and the smoak of the lime kilns, are altogether sublime,' wrote Arthur Young.[6] Joseph Wright of Derby made a famously dramatic painting (1780) of Arkwright's cotton mill by night, with trees silhouetted against the gloomy sky.

But by 1795, writing his *General View* of Lancashire for the Board of Agriculture, John Holt reported that 'capitals, labour, ingenuity and attention'[7] were all diverted away from farming and towards industry. In Lancashire, reckoned at that time to be the most heavily industrialised county in Britain, they produced cotton, silk and wool in factories employing spinners, bleachers, weavers, dyers, printers and tool-makers. They made hats, stockings, pins, needles, nails, earthenware, porcelain, watches and clocks. There were works for smelting iron and copper, works for casting plate glass and for making white lead, lamp black and vitriolic acid. Consequently, 'the growth of grain is annually and gradually on the decrease. The importation from foreign countries is, of course, upon the advance.'[8] There was little grazing land and meat had to be brought in from Westmorland or Durham, Yorkshire or Derbyshire. By 1810, Uvedale Price, champion of the picturesque, was writing, 'When I consider the striking natural beauties of such a river as that at Matlock, and the effect of the seven-storey buildings that have been raised there, and on other beautiful streams, for cotton manufactories, I am inclined to think that nothing can equal them for the purpose of disbeautifying an enchanting piece of scenery.'[9] And by 1854, when Charles Dickens published *Hard Times*, the effect on the landscape of the manufactories that Young had found so thrilling was already becoming hideously apparent: Coketown, where *Hard Times* was set, was 'a town of machinery and tall chimneys, out of which interminable serpents of smoke trailed themselves for ever and ever, and never got uncoiled. It had a black canal in it, and a river that ran purple with ill-smelling dye, and vast piles of building full of windows where there was a rattling and a trembling all day long, and where the piston of the steam-engine worked monotonously up and down like the head of an elephant in a state of melancholy madness.'[10]

W. G. Hoskins' book was the first comprehensive history ever written of the English landscape, but it ended on a pessimistic note. Since the beginning of the First World War, he wrote, every single change in the English landscape had either 'uglified' it or destroyed its meaning, or both. Over the countryside droned, day after day, 'the obscene shape of the atom-bomber, laying a trail like a filthy slug upon Constable's and Gainsborough's sky'.[11] And yet he acknowledged that this same landscape, shaped to a great degree by more than a thousand years of human activity, was the richest historical record we possess. In it, we can discover things for which no written documents exist, or have ever existed. In a walk of only a few miles, he wrote, 'one would touch nearly every century in that long stretch of time'.[12]

PART THREE

PROSPECTS AND PLACE

Surely it is time to recognize not a standard
of living but a standard of values, in which beauty
comeliness and the possibility of solitude have a
high place among human needs?

Jacquetta Hawkes, *A Land* (1950)

Howard Phipps, *Eggardon* (2007)

CHAPTER 14

A Particular Patch

I N DORSET TRICKS of history and geology have left the county unusually free of people and large towns. Or motorways to get to them. In the main, this remains a deeply rural landscape, where the burial mounds of the Bronze Age people living here in 2000 BC and the hill forts of the Iron Age people who succeeded them still remain the most dramatic features. The highest of the old camps is Lewesdon, at 915 feet, but the most powerful is surely Eggardon, with ramparts and ditches snaking round its sides in vertiginous loops. These are not natural features. They were made by men, hacking into the chalk with antler picks, and shovels made from shoulder blades. On a summer evening, the ghosts of these people, some of the earliest occupiers, lift out of the landscape, as long shadows pick out the lines of the tiny fields they made and the banked enclosures surrounding the farmhouses they built. At Turnworth, in the high empty country west of Blandford, you can even make out the narrow track leading away from the farmhouse to the pastures where, even then, goats and sheep and cattle were being kept.

These high chalk downlands, stretching right across Dorset, almost to Bridport in the west, create a particular type of landscape, quite different to the rich, profitable clay valleys of the Blackmoor Vale to the north. To the east are flat, acid heathlands, Hardy's Egdon Heath, 'the untameable,

Ishmaelitish thing' as he described it in *Return of the Native*. 'Civilisation was its enemy,' he wrote, 'and ever since the beginning of vegetation its soil had worn the same antique brown dress.'¹ Jutting out into the sea on the east is Purbeck, a place of quarries so particular in the stone they produced that, when we needed slabs to repair a roof, the surveyor could tell just from looking at an old slab exactly which seam it and its fellows had come from. At his request, two old men reopened the seam and cut new stone, which once a week we ferried across to the thirteenth-century dovecote we had inherited in a delicate state of collapse. It took our roofers just a day to lay what the quarrymen had taken a week to win from Purbeck's stony mass. At the end of the project, twentieth-century slabs lay alongside thirteenth-, fifteenth- and eighteenth-century slabs, testament to an unbroken tradition of building with the superb stone that underpins the landscape both at Purbeck and on Portland.

We live, not at Purbeck, but in the far west of Dorset and, naturally, it is the bit I love best. It's a place of small farms (there never were big estates in this part of Dorset, as there were up on Cranborne Chase), deep valleys each with its own busy stream, steep grassy hillsides, patches of wood thick with alder and hazel. Very narrow lanes with high sides embanked with ferns and primroses. Rough hedges which, from early spring, mark out the fields in a billowing succession of white blossom – first blackthorn, then hawthorn, then elder. Plenty of sheep. Boggy land at the bottom of the valleys where purple marsh orchids grow alongside ragged robin and rushes. A landscape where, as R. S. Thomas wrote about Wales,

> there are jewels
> To gather, but with the eye
> Only. A hill lights up

Suddenly; a field trembles
With colour and goes out
In its turn; in one day
You can witness the extent
Of the spectrum and grow rich
With looking[2]

Beyond 'our' valley lies the sea, though thankfully I cannot see it. All I need are the glimpses which our up-and-down land-scape occasionally allows – a sliver of silver shining between the steep sides of a valley. It's close, but not too close. From the house in West Dorset where we lived for forty years or so, where the children grew up, I could hear the waves at night, crashing on the banked-up pebble profile of Chesil Beach, as regular as breathing, hear the muffled fracturing of the water as it met the land, the rattle of the pebbles being dragged back into the undertow, to be overtaken once more by a fresh wave rearing, advancing and splintering on the shore. Two of our daughters were married from that house. When, after the first of the weddings, all the guests had gone, I walked across the lawn into the trees which lay on our boundary. We'd lit them up for the occasion, big old beech trees mostly, now stretch-ing their shadows at two o'clock in the morning across the lawn, across the tent, where we'd been noisily celebrating the marriage of the new bride, towards the house which for twenty-five years or so had been her home. By the stone bound-ary wall, in the deep quietness, the sound of the sea gradually filled all the space in my head, its metronomic rhythm, its vast intake and outtake of breaths, wiping out any sense of human time. Time past. Time to come. All subsumed in the sea's own inexorable timetable.

Dorset has a long stretch of coast, though as a seaside destina-tion, I'd describe it as low key. It's the place that westward-bound holidaymakers drive through on their way to 'proper' holiday destinations in Devon and Cornwall. And those of us who live in the place have mostly been content to be left to our own devices. So it was a shock to find the coast just a mile from our house unexpectedly designated as a World Heritage Site. UNESCO, who are responsible for making these decisions, included it then among four new sites in Britain: the industrial landscapes of the Derwent Valley Mills in Derbyshire, Saltaire in West Yorkshire, New Lanark in South Lanarkshire. And us, the Jurassic coast, as it is now being called, the first natural landscape in England to be designated in this way. It's become our equivalent of the Grand Canyon, our answer to the Great Barrier Reef (both also World Heritage Sites). Fortunately it has had relatively little effect. Visitors are, if they plan their visit carefully, still allowed to take on this staggering coastline in their own way, rather than have it interpreted for them. There seems to be rather little that we are allowed to discover now, without some notice board looming up to tell us how to look, how to decode. Interpretation of this kind is death to a natural landscape.

When I look out over that coast, or the mountains round the place where I was born in Wales, I'm not thinking geology, geomorphology, Triassic, Jurassic or Cretaceous. My response is immediate, visceral. The land rearing up, plunging down, the mist lying heavy in the valleys, the alternating blocks of plough and pasture, smudges of copse, sandstone cliffs swooping into the waves, an odd beam of brilliant sunlight boring a hole in the sea, all these things give joy. One sure way to dissipate the immediacy of that response is to have the place littered with signs: Welcome to the Jurassic Coast, Home of the Dinosaurs. With landscape, you first need to be hooked. Then, later, you can engage with the place on your own terms, find out what you want to know, rather than be force fed with the things that someone else has decided to tell you.

'New funding opportunities are already opening up,' said
Malcolm Turnbull, the Manager for Coast and Countryside
Policy at the time. 'We will now be looking at what further funding is available to us, in the light of the new status, which will
help us make the area accessible to all those who are interested
in visiting.' What could he have meant? We already have roads,
railways, even airports nearby at Southampton and Exeter. We
have car parks, excellent B&Bs. The many visitors who already
come don't seem to have trouble finding the place. They don't
stagger in, gaunt and emaciated, their water bottles empty.

Indeed, you'd have a problem missing it, since the new
World Heritage Site covers ninety-four miles, stretching from
Poole in the east to Exmouth in the west. It takes in the whole
of the Dorset coast, apart from the thickly developed area
round Bournemouth and Poole. It includes the fossil forest
near Lulworth where we used to take our children to gaze at
the dinosaur footprints padding round the vast boles of prehis-
toric trees. It embraces Charmouth beach, where after winter
storms we could pick up from the rock pools small ammonites
glistening with fool's gold. It's not what you'd call a welcoming coast. After Weymouth, boats sailing west are pushed to
find a decent anchorage until they reach Devon. We tried
mooring in Lyme Regis harbour once, but it was like riding a
giant dipper. We upped anchor in the middle of the night and
sailed on down to the more peaceful waters of the River Dart
at Dartmouth. Two thousand wrecks lie offshore.

You might have thought our new heritage status would bring
protection against unsuitable development. In terms of planning, the county (being an Area of Outstanding Natural Beauty
etc., etc.) is already one of the most restricted in Britain. Yet
over the past couple of years earth movers have been busy
reconforming the contours of one short stretch of this world-
class landscape to accommodate a new caravan site, a relief
road round Weymouth built for the Olympics (those fighting

against it eventually lost their appeal in the High Court) and a new golf clubhouse. All three may be necessary to sustain income and employment, but our visitors may wonder perhaps why developments are not more carefully designed to fit the existing landscape, rather than landscape being carved up to accommodate development.

Diversification is the way forward in rural areas, we are told. But this does not seem to mean producing a wider range of the foods that we presently import, at great cost to the balance of payments. It means theme parks, shooting ranges, off-road vehicle trails. And more golf courses. On the face of it, perhaps, a golf course does not seem too much of an intrusion in a rural landscape. It's still mostly green. But a modern golf course is no longer content to merge with the country in which it sits. All golf courses, wherever they are, try to look like Scotland. Landforms heave like schools of whales across lowland pasture, trying to pretend they are the Cairngorms. Conifers are planted in landscapes that, left to themselves, would never include a Scots pine.

The same *folie de grandeur* infects the clubhouse. It is pleasant to be able to get a drink after a game. Changing rooms and lockers are par for the course. But you do not have to dress up these modest requirements in the guise of a 'resource centre' or 'entertainment complex'. The average eighteen-hole golf course takes up about 125 acres of land. That seems plenty, but few planning applications are now without added facilities such as a satellite holiday village, a tourist lodge or hotel. Or a conference centre. With these add-ons, you can cover more than 400 acres of countryside without anyone even noticing. Lined up behind any such proposal are the usual troupe of consultants, pre-programmed with politically correct arguments, which, at a touch of a button, they can disgorge into the debate. They are very familiar: 'enhancing

the countryside' . . . 'improving wildlife habitats' . . . 'providing employment for local people'. There is no way in which
a golf course set in an Area of Outstanding Natural Beauty
can be said to improve wildlife habitats. There is nothing
life-enhancing for a plant or animal on the average green or
fairway. As an environment, a golf course is a fascist state.
And a thirsty one. Golfers do not expect parched and cracked
greens in return for their subscriptions. The Countryside
Commission, the government's advisor on landscape and
conservation, has a brief to improve access to the countryside, but has taken a firm line on golf courses, spelling out
the fact that golf courses and Areas of Outstanding Natural
Beauty are contradictory concepts. Golf courses, it continues, should go where they can make a positive contribution to
the landscape. It has in mind reclaimed land, brownfield sites,
but this is not so appealing to potential developers. The effort
and cash required to turn a non-existent landscape into the
sort of place in which you might conceivably want to while
away a Sunday morning are far greater than that involved in
plundering an AONB.

Areas of Outstanding Natural Beauty were designated by
the government in 1949; Dorset's is one of thirty-three in
England. It covers nearly half (44 per cent) of the county,
stretching east from the Upper Axe Valley in Devon to the
Stour Valley near Blandford Forum. Pretty much anywhere
here, walking the magnificent web of footpaths that connect
hamlet with hamlet (footpaths always had a purpose), you
will pass through layers of landscape made by more than a
thousand years of occupation and use. The Celtic people, who
made the stupendous earthworks, were famously beaten in
battle by the Romans as they moved west to Exeter. You can
find Roman bricks built into the walls of the twelfth-century
church of St Candida and the Holy Cross at Whitchurch

Canonicorum, see the mosaics that decorated their fancy villas ('Incomers' snort the first-century locals). Were the descendants of some of those Romans among the victorious mob who fought off the Vikings who landed at Weymouth between 970 and 1025? The invaders' skeletons, young warriors of fighting age, were unearthed in a mass grave on Ridgeway Hill, decapitated to a man.

At the head of our valley are the two hamlets of North and South Poorton, named in the Domesday Book as thriving agricultural settlements. They still are. Evensong at the tiny, steepled church of St Mary – Oh Lord defend us from the dangers and the perils of the night – unfolds to a background of cows being milked in the yard opposite. Downstream, towards Powerstock, strip lynchets curve in parallel lines across the sides of some of the hills, evidence of a land hunger in medieval times as the flatter land began to run out. Wherever I walk, I am looking out at a handmade landscape, an intimate landscape, each wood with its own name, a landscape that provides a livelihood for the people who own it but also endless, everchanging delights for those who walk it.[3] Only half a mile from our house, I can plunge into a valley so thickly wooded, so steeply sided that I am completely absorbed into this one microcosm, all familiar landmarks gone. Every winter, floods remake the contours of the stream that flows muddily through the foot of the valley. Down here, protected against wind, the soft sound of the stream and the *karrick cachow, karrick cachow* of the partridges are the only noises you can hear. Down here, in autumn, you can pick up sweet chestnuts, lying thickly about in their prickly cases. But who planted them? They are thought to have been introduced into Britain by the Romans, but were most widely planted in the eighteenth and nineteenth centuries. Three people clasping hands could not reach their arms round the trunks of some of these trees, trunks twisting, like

barley sugar, with age. And you only see them in this particular
patch, just a square mile or so, between here and Netherbury.
In Burghley Park on the outskirts of Stamford, where we
rented a place for a time, the ancient sweet chestnuts were
planted to give winter fodder to deer. Is that why these are
here? Small groups of roe deer pass across our fields at dusk.

Somewhere down here in the valley there must once have
been a mill, for on 28 September 1696 Giles Hitt and John
Pupp drew up an inventory of the goods and chattels belonging to John Gale, late of Loscombe. The most valuable of his
possessions were his four feather beds, with their three cover-
lets and six pillows, worth £8 (£22,430). The table board in
the 'kitching' containing ten pewter dishes, two pots, four
brass pans, a warming pan, two skillets, a kettle and three
plates were valued altogether at £3 11s od (£9,952). Taken
together the miller's clothes, his sheets, his chests and coffers
and boxes, his joint stools, sideboard, cradle, looking glass,
barrels, pails and lumber were estimated to be worth £19 12s
6d (£55,010). But who played the 'one old paire of verginals'
found in the chamber over the kitchen? Did its reedy notes
ever join the music of the stream in this remote valley?

Records of manorial courts, deeds, documents charting acts
of enclosure and the tithe maps later produced for each parish
in the county people the landscape, make clear who owned
what and what they did with it. Read alongside the censuses,
the Enumerator's Schedules, which started in 1801, and were
produced every ten years from 1841 onwards, you can place
exactly where these people lived and how they earned their
living. West Dorset was unusual in the number of people who
owned their own land, who were not tenants paying rent.

The 1839 tithe map for Powerstock, Thomas Hardy's
Poorstock, marks out more than a thousand plots of land,
almost a third of them occupied by the people who owned

them. But there were as many owners, people who had perhaps just a copse or a single field, who rented them out to someone else in the village. The census shows that Powerstock, like most other rural communities, was to a great extent self-sufficient. There was a butcher and a baker, a thatcher and a basket maker, a carpenter, a stone mason and a blacksmith, a tailor as well as a tailor's apprentice, an innkeeper and a shopkeeper, a washerwoman, a nurse and a postman. A few marked their position as 'farmer', most were set down as 'Ag Lab' – agricultural labourers; even if they had a field of their own, this could not supply an income. The census tells you, too, that this was a society where few new people came from far away into the village. Or moved out. In the 1841 Census there is a column showing whether inhabitants had been born in the county. The answer is always yes. The names in the census – Gale, Hansford, Hine, Legg, Northover, Palmer, Pitcher – are still names you'll find in the local phone book. A few people in the census are labelled 'Ind' – of independent means – like Martha Webber, eighty years old when the 1841 census was taken. Her son, Richard (fifty-five), was the schoolmaster in the village. Only one man, William Chilcott, identifies himself as a yeoman, setting himself rather above the other men of the parish whose lives were bound up with farming. When the 1841 census was taken, he occupied forty plots of land, a usefully self-sufficient mix of meadow and pasture (fourteen plots) and arable (fourteen plots) as well as five orchards and two coppices which would provide hurdles and firewood. His brother rented even more land. They were the ones on whom the other labourers of the village depended for work.

As with the communal grazing on the sheep-leazes which John Claridge described in his *General View of the Agriculture in the County of Dorset*, the way the land was used, the landscapes that were created by this use, depended on a complex, mutual understanding between the users. How many of these 'understandings', these agreements, would have been written down? The tithe map for Powerstock shows a proliferation of willow beds following the course of the streams through the valley. You might have expected Richard Cousins (sixty-five) and his son, Richard (forty), both marked down as basket-makers in the 1841 census, to have owned perhaps one of these willow beds, which could not have been of high agricultural value. But they didn't. One, for instance, lot 1056, was owned by Margaret Kitson, another, lot 1058, by Henrietta Shuckburgh, though neither were listed as occupiers of the land. These lots were occupied (i.e. rented) by Robert Grant, who owned a house and garden in the parish, but no land. Nevertheless, he was building up quite a holding in the parish, renting an orchard here (lot 566), a parcel of arable there (lot 634), as well as a patch of pasture (lot 539) and the willow beds, for the harvesting of which he would have made a charge to the basket-makers. That tiny web connected five people, but it could not have been spun without trust between neighbours with long memories and a deeply embedded understanding of how a landscape worked in a practical sense: what paths you could take to get to your fields; where exactly the boundaries lay in the strips of a common field. Remnants of the common fields established from medieval times onwards still show up in the mid-nineteenth century tithe map with strips divided not only between owners, but between parishes too. You also needed to be able to judge how likely a neighbour was to wait for rent until you could pay it.

The tithe map for Powerstock is rather plain. Some maps colour in the plots according either to ownership or to how the land was used at the time, which gives a more immediate understanding of the way the landscape might have looked. In terms of use, the land is divided into arable, pasture, meadow (two separate categories which we tend now to conflate), rough pasture, which included common land, orchard, wood and 'firs'. There were only a few small plantations of firs, all except one of them less than an acre in extent and nearly all owned by the Reverend Jenkins (his work in the parish seems to have been carried out by a curate that the census shows was living in the vicarage). He could doubtless afford to be the innovator, the instigator of practices, new then and only adopted in a manner that really impinged on the landscape in the vast conifer plantations set in train by the Forestry Commission in the 1930s.

In this 1839 tithe map, arable emerges as the biggest category, 991 acres held in 231 plots. This was perhaps brought about by the demand for hemp in the rope and net industry at nearby Bridport. Now, you'd say that pasture was the dominant feature in this green, hilly parish. In 1839, pasture came second place, occupying 859 acres held in 191 plots. The meadow plots were generally smaller – on average 2.8 acres against 4.5 acres, but there were more of them, 227 plots in all. Rough pasture covered 331 acres, most of that accounted for by the wastes (289 acres) of Powerstock Common. As for orchards, though collectively they covered no more than thirty-seven acres, there were masses of them – 113 separate plots, averaging less than a third of an acre each. These would have been primarily cider orchards (cider being part of the wages of many agricultural labourers), still shown as prominent features on the twenty-five inch to the mile Ordnance Survey map of 1903. Recently, under the inspired leadership of local builder, Nick Poole, cider-making has again become a defining feature of this particular area. Old orchards, like that at nearby Muddicombe, where in early May sheep graze under ancient trees swathed in pale pink blossom (a Samuel

Palmer landscape), are no longer being grubbed out. Woods on the Powerstock tithe map are largely accounted for by small coppices of less than an acre, most of them separately owned, which would have consisted chiefly of hazel and ash, both indispensable in a rural community that needed spars for thatching, material for hurdles, handles for scythes, beanpoles and pea sticks for their gardens.

Field names, listed on tithe maps such as the one made for Powerstock, are witnesses to the continuity that marks the gradual occupation of land in Britain, for it is the fields that make our landscape so intimate, so diverse, so particular. The patchwork you look down on from a plane when you are returning from somewhere else is the only proof you need that you are coming home. There is nothing like it anywhere else in Europe, in the world. The names on the Powerstock map are as varied as the landscapes they combine to create: Puzzicks, thirty-four acres of rough pasture owned by the Reverend Jenkins; Flinty Nap, nineteen acres of pasture and arable suggesting plough-breaking work for its owner, Abel Whittle; Bellringer's Orchard, which immediately brings to mind a scene from *Under the Greenwood Tree*.

In the field names are embedded clues to the way they had been, or continued to be used: Bean Close, Cowleaze, Roper's Quarry, Marl Pits, Hop Yard, Pig's Plot. Some (I would guess more recent) names indicate a field's size: Long Six Acres. Some names highlight the characteristic of a particular field: Well Plot, Lime Kiln Plot, Yellow Clays, Starvelands, Marsh Mead. Some make clear its owner, past or present: Hodge's Plot, Daniel's Mead. Some pinpoint a situation: Hither Broadleys, Yonder Broadleys, North Hemplands, South Hemplands. Some names – Foans, Drang – sound as if they have escaped from *Gawain and the Green Knight*.

The text that accompanies the tithe map is laid out in orderly columns, listing plot by plot the owner, occupier, type of land and extent, measured in acres, rods and poles. Together with the extra information provided by the census taken just two years later, you can start to fill the landscape with some of the people that were here before us. It's just one snapshot, one moment in time, but now whenever I walk past a field called Long Strap, perched high above steep banks and bounded on two sides by narrow lanes, I think of Absalom Guppy, who owned it in 1839. It was all the land he had, lot 342, consisting of two acres of arable. I tracked him only because of his mellifluous surname, known in West Dorset since the twelfth century (and still surviving), and learned that he'd been born c. 1803 in nearby Netherbury, where his father had a shop. At the age of twenty-six, in Powerstock Church, he had married Hannah Bailey, who was the same age as he was, but who already had two sons, John and James. By the time of the 1851 census he was forty-eight, living in West Milton, close to Powerstock, where John worked as a shoemaker. Absalom Guppy's occupation was given as haggler, which Henry Mayhew defined as 'the middle-man who attends in the fruit and vegetable markets and buys off the salesman to sell again to the retail dealer or costermonger'.[4] In the house with Absalom and Hannah at the time of the census were sons Thomas (fifteen), Absalom (ten), Robert (seven), William (six), Joseph (four) and daughters Hannah (thirteen), Harriet (eleven) and Maria (one) as well as the two boys from Hannah's previous marriage. By the time of the 1861 census, just two of the girls (Hannah and Maria, Hannah now working as a dressmaker, Maria listed as a 'scholar') and two of the boys (Absalom and Joseph) were still living in the West Milton house with their parents.

So why, ten years later, by the time of the 1871 census, was Absalom Guppy, aged sixty-eight, in the hated Stoke

Union, the workhouse on the outskirts of Beaminster (it has now been turned into a series of retirement flats)? He was one of nineteen men there, most of whom are described as agricultural labourers. He's also described as a widower, but he wasn't. Absalom's death was registered at the Stoke Union on 8 October 1872. His wife died ten years later, aged eighty, and was buried at the Holy Trinity church in Beaminster, by which time the severe depression that struck agriculture between the 1870s and 1914 was really beginning to affect those whose lives depended on the land. Occasionally, I walk the boundaries of Absalom Guppy's field, still arable, which is not surprising, for the soil is good. The land slopes gently to the south-west, surrounded by mixed hedgerows of ash, hawthorn, hazel, blackthorn, sycamore, bramble and elder. Bracken and comfrey lap in from the verges. In the top right-hand corner there's a big old ash tree, big enough perhaps to have been around when Guppy was working his land. What did he grow here? Potatoes? That's the most likely thought that occurred to me. To grow corn would have involved hiring in labour and I don't get the impression he was ever in a position to do that. Flax was profitable, but again, needed skilled people to harvest it. This is a small field. Guppy had a family of ten children. But he owned this land. That was the thing. That fact must have represented a kind of status in the community in which he lived. There's a fantastic view from the top of the field, but I feel almost guilty in enjoying it. Was he ever able to look out on a sunny day at the end of March when the ground was at last beginning to dry out and enjoy, as a positive pleasure (as I do), the landscape laid out in front of him: Gravel Hill and Browns Hill to the right, Mangerton Hill and grassy Round Knoll to the south, and beyond that a glittering sliver of the sea?

Gwen Raverat, *Village Green, Summer* (1935)

CHAPTER 15

Thomas Hardy's Wessex

THOMAS HARDY'S WESSEX, spread over the endpapers of the handsome Greenwood editions of his novels, covered an area much bigger than Dorset itself. But no other writer is so closely associated with the place, or has embedded his writing so deeply in the landscape that it becomes – it is a cliché now – a more powerful presence in his novels than their protagonists. In Dorchester, the county town, there's a statue of him close to the Top o' Town roundabout. Occasionally a wilting posy lies at his feet. More often, the statue is surrounded by a crowd of Japanese tourists, taking photographs of each other standing next to the Grand Old Man of English letters. In Japan, apparently, there is a Hardy society as thriving as the one in Dorset itself. He evidently strikes a chord in that culture, matches some trait in the Japanese soul.

If you are starting from Japan, Dorset is a long way to come on a pilgrimage and I sometimes wonder what the visitors make of what they find. The superb museum will not disappoint and the town itself is still exceedingly handsome, despite the hideous depredations of the last decade. Particularly good is the façade of Trenchard's house, which you can admire from Trinity Street. But the office in South Street where Hardy worked briefly as an architect is now marooned above an unlovely café. And then there is the problem of Max Gate, where Hardy lived for more than forty years.

Max Gate was designed by Hardy himself and built by his brother in the 1880s. It was there he wrote *Tess, The Woodlanders* and *Jude the Obscure*, but as a key to understanding Hardy or his work the place reveals nothing except the rightness of his decision to make his way as a writer rather than as an architect. It is a staggeringly ugly house of plum brick with two corner turrets and a dark slate roof. It is about as gloomy and badly built a place as you could hope to find in Dorset, where you have to work quite hard to find an old house that is ugly. The lack of any aesthetic or architectural interest would not matter if you felt that by seeing the house you understood the man and his work better. Here you do not. All the grandeur of the prose, the touching resonance of the poetry rebound uselessly against the brick boundary wall of this unpleasant place.

Of course, as a way of reading a personality, shrine visiting is no more worthwhile than reading *Hello!* We can dress it up with as much intellectual pretension as we like: 'Meaningful Brickwork in the Novels of Thomas Hardy', 'Architecture as a Window on the Soul', 'The Face at the Casement, the Legs on the Stair'. In the end, we come to a shrine to pull a great person down to our less elevated level. We peer at his favourite chair, tell ourselves we have one just like that at home, we gaze at a random jumble of china and glass and walking sticks which in all probability meant as little to the person in question as they do to us. The things that are really important, we wear out. It is only the best, the scarcely used china that survives and the stick that you never take out with you on your walks.

As it happens, there is not even the china or the walking sticks at Max Gate. There is very little. The contents of the house were sold after the death of Hardy's second wife. The house itself was bought at auction by his devoted sister, Kate, who in 1940 gave it to the National Trust. But the famous study she left in its entirety to Dorchester's fine museum. Many other artefacts, bookcases, books, Hardy's own drawings and paintings, also found their way there. If you want to goggle at Hardy's Stilton scoop or search for significance in his shaving mug (a particularly hideous object, Staffordshire earthenware of a vile shade of pink), that is where you have to go.

James Lees-Milne, then the Trust's historic buildings representative, paid an unwilling visit to Max Gate in 1947. 'Perfectly hideous and shapeless,' he wrote in his diary. 'Shoddily built, with lean-to odds and ends added by him. It will be a constant expense. I shall advise the Historic Buildings Committee to sell it – it is held alienably – and keep the money for buying the birthplace which is far worthier.'[1] John Fowles, the novelist, a more recent pilgrim, was equally disappointed. 'There is, I think, no greater shock in English literary biography than to go round that far from distinguished villa just outside Dorchester, set on its rather bleak upland . . . We come expecting the palace of a maker of a fabulous kingdom, and are faced with a brick mediocrity, more suitable to a successful local merchant of his time than anything else.'[2]

Determined pilgrims need to abandon the town and take to the countryside, where, in a walk of no more than five miles, you can take in birthplace, school, family graves and the settings for several novels. From the Thorncombe Wood nature reserve at Higher Bockhampton a trail leads through the wood to Hardy's birthplace (which the Trust did buy – in 1948). The house is pretty much what you would hope: small, thatched, tucked under a bank with beech trees crowding round behind. Then make for Stinsford church, where part of Hardy is buried. The rest of him is in Poet's Corner, Westminster Abbey, which is a poser for pilgrims. Where do you leave the flowers? I suppose it depends on which you consider the most important part of the body. Hardy's heart is here, buried in the coffin of his first wife, Lavinia Gifford.

The whole macabre episode could have been written by Hardy himself: the surgeon's flashing knife, the opening of the grave, the onlookers at the graveside.[3] And then, hovering over all, is the irony that united in death (symbolically at least) were a couple who in life seemed to have very little to say to each other. The Hardy graves are heavy, coffin-shaped structures, not a patch on the superbly lettered headstones of earlier generations of the family. Or on Cecil Day Lewis's slate memorial, only a few yards away. The church, dedicated to St Michael, is splendid, mostly thirteenth century, with a Saxon relief of the saint, wings powerfully outspread, on the outside of the tower.

A lane leads down past the churchyard and brings you out on a causewayed footpath with streams either side making their way to the River Frome. Wandering along this path with clear, swift water running over shallow pebble beds, roofed over with laurel, holly and yew, you are at the heart of the now-forgotten system of water meadows that was once an important feature of this landscape. Already by 1608, complicated agreements were being drawn up by four tenants on the Ilsington estate near Puddletown to flood meadows alongside the River Frome by way of a channel 900 yards long and seven foot wide. Henry Arnold, the new owner of Ilsington, was a great promoter of this new, though complex, technique, which made it possible to flood meadows artificially with the aim of encouraging early spring grass. From his neighbour, Henry Hastings, he secured a licence that enabled him 'to erect Weares and bays athwart the river for watering their grounds so that no damage is done or cattle drowned'. Fortunately, Hastings was equally keen on the idea and in 1629 was encouraging his tenants to create new water meadows on the Broadmoor at Puddletown. These

Dorset schemes were the first of their kind in England and inevitably there were arguments: about rights to water, about access routes for stock, about the cutting of new channels.[4] Nevertheless, the innovation was widely copied, especially in the neighbouring counties of Wiltshire and Hampshire. Puddletown, close to Hardy's birthplace, became even more renowned after the publication in 1779 of a pioneering work, *On Watering Meadows*, by the local agent, George Boswell.

By 1793, giving his *General View of the Agriculture in the County of Dorset*, John Claridge estimated that there were an astonishing 50,000 acres of water meadows in Dorset, providing extra grazing for the ever increasing numbers of sheep that brought the county its prosperity. 'The proportion of water meadows is nowhere so great, or anywhere better managed,' he wrote. 'The early vegetation produced by flooding is of such consequence to the Dorsetshire farmer that without it their present system of managing sheep would be about annihilated.'[5] All the major river valleys – the Piddle, the Frome, the Stour – were criss-crossed with dykes and ditches, and the rivers punctuated with weirs to flood the land.

Work on the meadows started at Christmas, after cattle had grazed down the grass. All the channels and the hatches that controlled the flow of water were put into good repair before the water was 'thrown over' the meadows from one channel to the next. This kept the frost out of the ground during the cold months and encouraged the early spring grass that made Dorset's farmers pre-eminent in the market for early lambs. The gradients of the channels were 'so well taken care of', observed Claridge, that water never lay stagnant on the land. Huge effort was put into the infrastructure. The meadows were grazed from March until the first or second week in May. By then, the grass on the high open sheep-leazes would be ready for grazing. Then the water meadows were watered again to encourage a flush of new grass that could be taken off as a hay crop in late June or early July. Water meadows produced twice as much hay as unwatered ones and you'd get your crop without having to worry about a summer drought. After hay-making was over, the meadows were sometimes watered a third time to produce grass for the cattle that grazed there from early September to Christmas.[6] Hardy described the meadows in *The Return of the Native* as 'watered on a plan so rectangular that on a fine day they look like silver gridirons'.[7] No 'drowners' work these waterways now, but ambling through this curious landscape, you marvel at the industry that created it all.

The path eventually emerges at Lower Bockhampton by a three-arched brick bridge where a pair of swans often hover, stemming the flow. Hardy went to school in this village, for a short time at least, until his ambitious mother thought he would do better at Mr Last's academy in Dorchester. The final objective, Hardy's Egdon Heath, now lies in front and slightly to the right of you, the western edge of the acid heathland that rolls over to Wareham and beyond. West of Dorchester, you do not get heath names. Places are marked by hill and down. East of the town, the country changes dramatically. Duddle Heath and Puddletown Heath, which became part of Hardy's Egdon, stretch on through a score of heath names until the country changes again to the south with the violent geological eruptions of Purbeck.

The farm track of Pine Lodge Farm brings you out on to the heath, mostly dressed now in forestry green, as silent and impenetrable a form of clothing as was ever invented. There is some heath, but it is heavily trailed. No sooner have you whipped yourself up into a wild, Eustacia Vyeish frame of mind than you come nose to nose with a visitor information board telling you all you need to know about beetles. It is a common enough conflict of interests. Let the beetles have this emasculated patch and push on through the woods past the pond, back to Hardy's cottage and your starting point. There is wild country still in Dorset, but it is not here. You need to go east of Wareham to the heaths of Arne, Middlebere, Slepe and Stoborough to discover what this tract of land might once have been. Even while Hardy was writing the Wessex novels, the world he was describing no longer existed. The railway had come to Dorchester in 1847. By 1866 one of the first steam ploughing engines ever seen in the county was breaking up old downland at Alton Pancras, not far north of where he grew up. Before Hardy was even born, the counterparts of the amiable agricultural labourers of his early novel, *Under the Greenwood Tree*, had in fact fought bitterly to establish the first union of labour at Tolpuddle, only eight miles or so away from his birthplace, and had been transported to Australia for their pains. The landscape of the Wessex novels is the country of Hardy's grandparents. Hardy, living in a time of violent transition and rural depopulation, was looking back nostalgically to a time when order had seemed eternal.

Given this, it is odd that so much of the literature on Hardy is preoccupied with minutiae. Here Sergeant Troy spent the night in the church porch (Puddletown). There the d'Urbervilles set up their four-poster bed (Bere Regis). There Giles Winterbourne in *The Woodlanders* stood with his apple tree (Sherborne). The problem with this sort of approach is that you can become so obsessed with ticking off the notes, you do not hear the tune. The landscapes that Hardy conjures up in the Wessex novels are atmospheric, impressionistic landscapes, not documentary facsimiles. Of course he was influenced by his surroundings, but it suited his dramatic purpose not to mention that large parts of his literary Egdon had in fact been enclosed by squatters or Acts of Parliament.

It does not matter whether the woods that Hardy was describing in *The Woodlanders* are in the Blackmoor Vale or not. He is evoking the archetypal wood, 'roots whose mossed rinds make them like hands wearing green gloves; elbowed old elms and ashes with great forks'. And then, because we must not run away with the idea that woods are nice places to be in, 'The lichen ate the vigour of the stalk and the ivy slowly strangled to death the promising sapling.'[8] Each novel has its own landscape, which is chosen and tailored to meet specific needs. That landscape sets the mood of the novel, enmeshes its characters, even becoming part of them, like the reddle-man stained with earth ochres in *The Return of the Native*, or Giles Winterbourne 'leafy and smeared with green lichen'. The woodland is constructed, as are all Hardy's landscapes, to illustrate the futility of man's endeavour.

This is not to say that you cannot learn about Dorset from Hardy's novels. Of course you can. He had a countryman's eye, untrammelled by all the baggage of a university educa-tion. Contours of land, soils, crops, methods of work, spring flowers, 'fern sprouts like bishop's croziers, the square-headed moschatel, the old cuckoo-pint, like an apoplectic saint in a niche of malachite'[9] are there observed in the closest detail. More important, though, in understanding the landscape, here, as anywhere else, is what he was saying about larger matters: man's relationship to the land, nature's indifference to cruelty, the sensation of time as well as space that is locked into the land – 'the many gay charioteers, now perished, who have rolled along the way, the blistered soles that have trodden it and the tears that have wetted it'.[10]

For these messages to be heard, however indistinctly, you need to be on foot, not hurtling round the Tess Trail, notching off the landmarks on the dashboard of your car. Fight your way in winter along the winding sweep of Chesil Beach, with the sea pounding savagely on the shore, grinding and gnashing the pebbles with monstrous force. Walk over the Celtic hill fort at Eggardon, home of the Celts before the Romans ever came this way. Harebells litter the short turf in summer and the land drops away in a giddying swoop to the woods of Powerstock Common. Climb through the beech woods of beautiful Lewesdon, west of Beaminster. On a late May day when the hill is carpeted with bluebells and woodpeckers and jays shriek at each other from the trees, you may think there is nowhere more harmonious on earth. Yet here, one day, out of a bright blue sunny sky in April came a blizzard borne on a wind so terrifying that I threw the children on the ground and cowered over them, expecting that at any moment we would be subsumed into the chaos, fragments of a much darker, more disturbing world than the one we thought we inhabited. Nature's indifference is more than a literary construct.

Howard Phipps, *Malacombe Bottom* (2010)

CHAPTER 16

What Does Landscape Offer?

W HAT DO WE assume is offered in that word 'land-scape'? The *OED* carefully suggests 'a view or prospect of natural inland scenery, such as can be taken in at a glance from one point of view'.[1] So hills, valleys, streams, rocks, trees might all be part of the prospect, but the definition, by the use of that word 'natural', seems to exclude many of the things that give me pleasure in a landscape: grazed pasture, the network drawn out over the land by the lines of hedges, the changing patterns of ploughed land as bare earth gives way to the first green growth, drifting slowly through the summer towards the buff-yellow of ripening corn. After that, stubble, then plough again, the earth ridged and furrowed, bossed into parallels. For me, a landscape wholly untouched by man is not automatically better than one that has evolved over centuries of labour. Vital to both is the sky: the contrast with the land, the movement of clouds through it (the movement of clouds is always mesmerising), the position of the sun in it, the infinity of the sky compared with the finite horizons of the land.

So, the dictionary does not suppose that any old stretch of land makes a landscape. It has to give us a view, a view more-over that we can take in 'at a glance'. It presupposes some kind of physical or mental framing, some instinctive editing of the kind we do when we use a proper camera with a view-finder. That of course doesn't find views. It just helps us to recognise when the elements we're being offered sit together in what seems to us a pleasing way. It's a view framer. William Gilpin was rigid in the rules he laid down for a 'correct' view, but the way we respond to a landscape doesn't have anything to do with rules. It's intuitive. Aesthetic, too, of course. There are thrilling landscapes in the Highlands, and I go there every autumn to be terrified, pulverised by the force of the mountains, ecstatic. But living on a high like that can't be sustained. By upbringing, background, character, I am predisposed to softer hills, more pastoral views. The way the hills of West Dorset fold into each other, dark pools of trees breaking up the paler green of pasture, these are the quiet landscapes that sustain me. Johnson Grant, travelling in 1797 through the Lake District, delighted in the fact that in the further reaches he found 'no disturbing traces of cultivation'.[2] Here in the West Country, those same traces add greatly to my delight.

There's a gateway on the lane that leads out of our valley to the bigger road at Melplash. And there, over the rails of the gate, is a view that stops me every time I drive the lane. It's not one of those ooh-aah views that stopped – still stop – tourists in the Lakes or the highlands of Scotland. It's a quiet view, but the texture of the rounded hills, now scarcely more than 100 feet high, ground down from the mountains they once were by millions of years of rain and wind, the way the pastures roll quietly down into the valleys, the small copses of trees, the way the light of early morning and early evening casts different shadows down the slopes, all these calm, soft movements of and on the land offer peace. Solace. Engagement. A slow-burning joy. I feel I belong in this landscape, that I'm part of it, almost. This is a view that welcomes you into, rather than separates you from, the land. That's not how it is with the big views, the kind marked on brown tourist signs. There, the landscape is something beyond. You are not part of it. It is too big. The new brings sharper shocks, but here, in the view over the gate, is a more enduring intimacy.

Certain things about it can be pinned down. I'm looking due south, to within a degree. The compass tells me that. I can locate the view on an Ordnance Survey map and give it an OS reference number. I can name the hills I'm looking out on: the smooth hump of Hincknoll Hill immediately to the right, Bull's Hill rising outside my view on the left. The dark vortex of the view is Hincknoll Coppice, a mixture of hazel and wild cherry oak, sycamore and thorn. Beyond, on the right, run the three humps of Mangerton Hill, Gravel Hill and the smooth flat top of Brown's Hill. Over on the left, divided by the brook I know is there but can't see, there's the tumulus on Knight's Hill, and strip lynchets with the banks between them lined out in bracken. Far over on the edge of my view are the ramparts of Eggardon. The plateau of its summit marks the horizon, the limit of my view.

So this is the physical nature of it. These are its bumps and hollows, its folds and valleys. Innumerable springs rise on the sides of the hills, the hills themselves relics of some vast cataclysmic eruption in the Jurassic Age. But in a landscape that has been continuously occupied for thousands of years you absorb, unconsciously perhaps, much more than

the contours drawn out so painstakingly on the Ordnance
Survey map. There, the hills, flattened into two dimensions,
are drawn out like fingerprints. But though the fundamentals
of this landscape are givens – the lie of the land, the earth that
underpins it, the water that carves it into small valleys and
bogs – what I'm absorbing also is the labour of the people that
have lived here. There are no houses in this view, no farms,
no barns even, but they exist, just over the brow of that hill,
just behind that clump of trees. As a landscape it bears few
marks of the Industrial Revolution, though the particularly
wide band of hedge that runs through the view, left to right,
marks a metalled road with the hedges set high on either side.
Crumbling stone lime kilns in the fields, rusting hydraulic
rams in the streams, the remains of a roughly constructed
sheep dip, speak of the constant effort to persuade the land
to provide a living.

In the main, the pattern of the fields is the same now as
it was when it was drawn out on the large-scale OS map of
1903, twenty-five inches to the mile. But the big square field
that pushes up the side of Mangerton Hill has arrived since
then, probably in the 1950s, when massive grants were paid
to farmers to clear ground and grow more food. It happened
on the bracken-covered sides of the hills where I grew up.
Dangerous ground, often, in terms of its steepness. Tractors
turned over. Farmers were crushed and killed. Typically, there,
when the grants dried up, the bracken returned. But this big,
square field was taken from pasture, not rough hillside, and is
still in cultivation – maize this year, the rows standing out on
the hill like green corduroy.

Time is stitched into this landscape – any landscape – but
time as measured by many different kinds of clock. Geologists
measure it in millions of years, the years that underpin what

I'm looking at now. Historians measure it in thousands of years, tracking the interventions between man and land, the making of those lynchets to provide more favourable growing ground, the damming of streams to provide water for cattle, the introduction of coppicing, the planting and laying of hedges, all these are woven into the landscape that I see over the gate. All can be approximately dated. The farmers' clock is set by the seasons, the inexorable roll of solstice and equinox that marks spring and summer, autumn and winter. Across this dash momentary interpolations: a rook on the wing, swooping over the view, wings trimmed back, riding the wave of air that we can scarcely sniff at but which is yet part of this view, this landscape. Like the clouds in the sky, birds in flight bring animation, difference, intrigue, enchantment, uplift to a scene.

This landscape, this view, is different every time I look at it, which is why it gives such enduring joy. It's a pleasure available to anyone. Views like this are free. But looking at a view is very different from looking at a painting of it. That, too, can give delight over and over again, though it never changes. But a landscape encapsulates change. Some, like the growth of the sycamore and the ash in the pasture opposite, are imperceptible. Some changes come suddenly, shockingly, as when a big, old, landmark tree is blown over in a gale. The flux is constant, though we don't register it. In terms of time, there's no beginning or end to a landscape. We set those markers ourselves, to render infinity less terrifying.

We set the beginning of our year in January, but if there is any beginning in the working landscape I look at over the gate, then I'd put it at Michaelmas, 29 September. Michaelmas, Christmas, Lady Day (25 March) and Midsummer Day are the Quarter Days fixed into our calendar since the Middle Ages.

They fall very close to the times of the summer and winter solstice (the longest and shortest days), and the two equinoxes, when day and night are of exactly the same length. These are not random dates.

Michaelmas is a kind of fulcrum in the farming year. The crops of the current year have mostly been gathered in (maize, a relatively new crop in Britain, comes later), and there's a brief pause before fields are ploughed and sown for the following season. It's the time when farm rents are paid, new leases drawn up, farms change hands. The landscape I look out at over the gate is poised and still, holding its breath in the way that only happens in early autumn. In the early morning, mists fill the hollows in diaphanous layers, trees and hills separated from each other by the gauzy ectoplasm. Sheep return to the pasture. It's a dream time. There is an element of lottery about these gorgeous days of late September and October. Nothing can be taken for granted. The spell will soon be broken. But when? Each day of still richness might be the last. The sun, lower in the sky now, throws long shadows even by mid-afternoon. The fact I'm looking south is one of the reasons this view constantly intrigues. The sun moves across it from left to right. The shadows swing round with it. Different elements of the landscape catch the light and for that moment, rise pre-eminent, then fall back as the sun moves on.

Butts for the shooters are set up on the nearest slope. Green seeps from the leaves of the big sycamore standing alone on the slope to the right. The rounded head of the oak at the edge of the copse below moves very slowly from dun green into a pale brown. The leaves are slow to drop. The larches in the copse to the left turn to a fox colour. By the time of the winter solstice, the trees stand bare, finer, more interesting in this skeletal state than they are fluffed about with leaves. Even by eight in the morning the sun has scarcely pulled itself up over Eggardon's plateau to bring light into the view over the gate. All is in shadow. By mid-afternoon it is once again lying back in shade, only the west-facing sides of the further hills still catching the low, slanting light from the sun as it moves towards its setting.

Paradoxically, it seems to me that the view over the gate is at its finest in winter. In composing any picture, the taking out is as important as the putting in. May is rich, with its froths of cow parsley and elegant croziers of fern, the brilliance of new grass and the sense of fecundity that the land breathes out at this time. But in winter, the land is reduced to its bones, and these are fine, ancient bones. Colour drains out, the lines of the hills, separated often by a line of mist between, are more strongly drawn. And as the land sinks into winter subfusc, colour bleeds across the sky at sunrise and sunset, burning pink and orange above while frost covers the slopes below.

Low winter light shows up features you don't see in summer, when the trees are bulky and the grass lush. Old tracks, hollows where stone has been dug out for building, the ridges made by sheep as they move across the slope, tumuli, burial mounds, disc barrows of the long dead. The land here holds the shapes of its past because there is very little arable ground. There have been few ploughs to smooth out traces of what has happened here. So in winter, I stop longer than I do in summer, peering out into this enigmatic composition of hills, looking always for things that in summer are not so easy to pick out. Looking, looking, feeling for the lives left behind on this land. Thinking of Absalom Guppy and his field, Long Strap, which lies at the end of the broad double hedges bordering the lane to West Milton. Thinking of Samuel Stevens and John Chilcott, who once farmed the fields low down in the valley where, in winter, the frost sometimes lies all day. Occasionally there's snow, which intensifies the monochrome nature of the view, disturbed only by the flashing, clattering flight of pheasant, taking unwillingly to the wing when I disturb them. Apart from them, there's little movement in the landscape: a tractor driver bringing fodder out to the sheep, rooks far away. Snow muffles sound, as well as detail. The pines planted on top of Hincknoll Hill stand out black against the sky.

The end of winter is marked by the mole, heaving up the detritus of his underground wanderings. The swooping slope of the pasture just over the gate is covered in lines of molehills. It's fine, beautiful earth; countrymen used to collect it for their seed sowing. Now it's left where it lies and provides a seedbed for vetch and pignut, buttercup and briar. Sometimes at this season the cloud hangs so low, it slices off the whole of the middle of the landscape. Dull, dun weather. But then, before the trees leaf up, the geans come into bloom in the Bull's Hill coppice. They make huge trees, these wild cherries, landmarks, when in bloom, for miles around. The greens intensify, especially the grass of the pasture. The sycamore standing alone on the slope to the left moves more slowly into life. At midday, it casts a neat shadow of itself on the ground, a perfect circle of branch and twig, each detail of this great standing object transfigured into two dimensions. This perfection of form doesn't last long. As the sun swings round in the sky, the tree shadow slithers round with it, lengthens, distorts, stretches down the slope until it is subsumed in the general shade of evening.

I sometimes pass the gate early on a May morning, soon after sunrise, and catch a sense of a world that has nothing to do with us: badgers, foxes, owls, bats, deer, ghosts inhabit and move freely about in this landscape when we are out of the way. Early in the morning you can hear separately each different bird in the dawn orchestra, blackbirds and robins doing their clarinet solos, wood pigeons droning on with the only phrase they know – 'You CAN'T go just now. You CAN'T go just now.' The landscape is very still, very poised. Black and white cattle have replaced sheep on the lush new grass of the pasture, but at this hour, even they are lying down.

It's mostly pasture, this landscape, too hilly for much else, but the big field carved out of the grassy side of Hincknoll Hill catches the eye now, freshly ploughed and drilled with maize. The long strip lying alongside the lane has been ploughed too and, for the short time before the crop greens them over again, these two shapes stand out as fiercely in the landscape as the rectangles of a Mondrian painting. John Chilcott who had that long strip would never have seen maize. Nor did I, growing up around my uncles' farms in the Border Country between England and Wales. Though it came into the country at the beginning of the twentieth century, it took a while before farmers trusted it. As a crop, it was used to more sun than we could give it over here. Being tender, you couldn't sow it before late May. Now that it's been coaxed into accepting a cooler climate and a shorter growing season, you see it all over southern England. It looks the same as sweetcorn, but the kernels are hard and starchy, not sweet. When it's harvested, the whole plant, the six foot stem, leaves as well as cobs, is cut, ground up in a macerator and stored in tall tower silos to be fed to cattle penned up in winter.

A tractor moves in to top off the wide sweep of pasture immediately beyond the gate, and marks out wide concentric semi-circles on the grass. Docks, thistles, nettles are cut down; coarse tussocks of grass are combed out. The marks last a surprisingly long time. The light is at its most gauzy and gorgeous in midsummer, the whole landscape periodically brushed over with the shadows of clouds passing above. I begin to wonder about the unusually flat top of Gravel Hill. It's not marked as a hill fort, but it would be well placed to pick up signals from the Celts living on Eggardon to the east and pass them on to the hill fort at Lewesdon to the west. This is dangerous territory. A Celt myself, I am too prone to see them rising up all around me, reminders that they were inhabiting this land for thousands of years before the Romans moved in.

The greatest variable in this (or indeed in any) landscape is the light. It epitomises the essential nature of landscape, that it is at the same time unchanging and ephemeral. But it is the most difficult thing to describe. The whole point of it is its fleetingness, its sudden brightness as R. S. Thomas describes:

> I have seen the sun break through
> To illuminate a small field
> For a while, and gone my way
> And forgotten it. But that was the pearl
> Of great price, the one field that had
> Treasure in it. I realize now
> That I must give all that I have
> To possess it.[3]

Morning and evening are best. Always. The angle at which light hits the land creates contrasts that are more vivid,

more moving than at any other time of the day. But by high
summer the foliage of the trees becomes almost sullen, the
light during the day is often too bright. This is not the best
time to look at the landscape I have in mind. Growth at the
verges of the fields is coarse and rank. The tractor driver
returns to fight bracken on the slope behind the sycamore.
It's too steep for him to move across the land. Instead he
reverses up the slope, cuts his way down, reverses back up
again, an arduous process, an ancient enemy. Left to itself
bracken would cover all these pastures, a bully of a plant
and therefore hugely successful. It was growing round here
55 million years ago, looking much the same then as it does
now. Or so the fossils suggest. Moving underground with
relentless rhizomes, it colonises land at hideous speed, pushing out plants that get in its way. It was cut as bedding on the
hill farms where I grew up, but as a foodstuff it's toxic. It
harbours sheep ticks too, which is another reason to get rid
of it. Ticks pass on Lyme Disease.

I try not to romanticise this landscape I look at almost every
day. My grandfather, my mother's father, left for America to
escape the great agricultural depression that hit Britain at the
end of the nineteenth century. Wheat that had been worth
seventy shillings a quarter was fetching just twenty-four shillings by 1894. He had with him a pedigree Herefordshire bull
and returned from the States in triumph with enough stud
money to sweep my Herefordshire grandmother off her rather
refined feet and bring her over the border to the family farm,
The Pant. The long succession of wet, cold springs and unpro-
ductive summers of that time, is part of West Dorset, too.
The landscape stores the memories away; adversity leaves its
marks, but over time the land repairs them. The sheep that
disappeared from these pastures in such vast numbers during

the depression, return again, wander again into the shade of the big sycamore where they always lie in the hottest part of the day. By the end of summer they've worn the ground round its trunk into an island of completely bare earth.

Gradually, towards the end of summer, the green slopes of the pasture are dusted over with creamy-pink as the grasses on the steepest banks come up into seed. The sheep don't like this tussocky dry stuff; they stay down on the lower ground that the tractor topped off. They are rarely given the best pickings. The cattle get that. But they are discriminating in their grazing; and in an old, established pasture, carefully select the grasses they like best. The landscape settles: soft, dreamy, half-asleep, like a Samuel Palmer painting. 'We must take the trouble to map out and paint with the different local colours arable land and garden, which come in every variety of rows and patterns,' he wrote, around 1850, to a pupil who was coming to join him on a painting holiday in North Devon.

> Also woods and woody hills must be juicy and rich; real TREE COLOUR, not anything picture colour. Detached elegant trees sometimes stand out into the glade; and above the woody or arable hill-tops, a bit of much higher hill is sometimes visible, all heaving and gently lifting themselves, as it were, towards the heavens and the sun. It is of no use to try woody hills without a wonderful variety of texture based on the modelling . . . WHAT CAN BE THE REASON that they delight so much? NEVER FORGET THE CHARM of running water. In Berryarbour valleys it gushes everywhere. O! the playful heave and tumble of lines in the hills here.[4]

Like a sheep, I am hefted now to the hills of West Dorset, the landscape I love best encapsulated in this unassuming view over the gate. The trees loom, darker green as the summer wears on. The greens of the pasture thicken. The shapes of the hills endure. Full. Still. At Michaelmas, I gaze once again into the misty distance beyond the final horizon of the land. It is evening and the sky is striped in layers of horizontal cloud. I can hear a pair of ravens calling to each other.

Samuel Palmer, *A Church among Trees* (c. 1830)

Ending

IN DORSET IS the landscape that for more than forty years has contained, surprised, delighted and occasionally terrified me. It is my chosen landscape. My chosen me. And yet, etched deep into my soul is the unchosen, the landscape into which I was born, where I started. That place will never go away, as I realised when, on a freezing winter morning, I went to an uncle's funeral, held at St David's, the small parish church of Llanddewi Rhydderch in Monmouthshire. An impenetrable fog lay over the countryside that day, reducing the trees on the edges of the churchyard to pale, stretching shadows. White frost rimed the skeletons of cow parsley. The fog muffled all the usual noises and when you breathed it, it tore a chill chasm down your throat.

A mile to one side of this church lies the farm where my uncle, my mother and their ten brothers and sisters were born and brought up. A mile to the other is the farm where he himself spent most of his working life. Farming neighbours, many of whom had been at school with my uncle seventy years before, crammed into the packed church in their dun-coloured British warm overcoats. The familiar tweed caps that rode with them on their tractors, accompanied them to the Tuesday markets, saw them through their Saturday nights at the pub, had disappeared. Their bare heads came as a shock.

In this same church my uncle and all his brothers and sisters had been baptised. My mother had been married here more than fifty years ago. So had several others among the dwindling band of aunts, now perched insubstantially in the front pews of the tiny building. The young priest, newly arrived in the parish, did not attempt a peroration. We sang 'Fight the Good Fight', with the strong Welsh tenors nursing the last notes of each verse, reluctant to let them go. A cousin read two poems from my uncle's favourite book, *Poets of the Landscape*. At the end of the service, his grandsons, farmers too, carried his coffin out of the church on their shoulders, swaying steadily over the uneven ground to the grave.

The earth here is the red earth that runs through all this border country into Herefordshire, where my grandmother was born. Heaped by the grave, it made the only slash of colour in the muffled, blanketed landscape. Slowly, we filed past it, scooping up fragments of the frozen earth to drop upon the coffin.

What comforted me at this funeral was its inevitability. There was no question about where and how my uncle should be buried. His belonging to this place, leading his life inextricably entwined in this particular landscape, lent a positive sense of fitness to his funeral. The life led unequivocally to the death, the burial in this familiar place. The earth that surrounded and supported him during his life subsumed him in his death.

This sense of fitness, of inevitability, is perhaps easier to achieve in country areas than in towns. Easier, too, in my uncle's generation than my own. We are a more rootless lot. Education, claustrophobia, marriage, work, a sense of adventure, a desire for freedom drive us increasingly away from our origins. We drift through our lives, no longer identifying ourselves with any particular landscape. We lose sight of where we came from. The price of this freedom is deracination. Where does this leave us when we die? The place matters, no matter how much you try and persuade yourself of the unimportance of the corporeal body.

Sometimes, though, you have a chance to shake off the neutering miasma of the crematorium. This is why, at half past four one morning in May, I found myself climbing over a dog and her new puppies to get to my brother's gun cupboard. It was a month or so after my mother's funeral. After the cremation her ashes had been locked in the cupboard while we decided what to do with them. The crematorium nearest to our home was in a town she never went to. That bothered me, perhaps to a disproportionate extent, and the experience had to be exorcised.

My brother could not talk about the subject. Nor could my father. But I had woken that May morning with the absolute conviction that I knew what to do. Carrying the ashes, still in the crematorium's black plastic bag, I walked up the lane towards the mountains where all my childhood was spent. I passed the small valley where my mother and I often had picnic teas. I passed the place where we picked winberries every August. I crossed over the path that led to the globe-flowers and the wild orchids to which we made a pilgrimage each spring.

Just here my dog, who was with me, put up a fox and the two animals streamed liquidly around the foot of the mountain I was climbing, the fox's tawny back melting into last year's bracken. It was fully light by now and sunny and windy. It took two hours to climb to the top of the Sugar Loaf, a route I had taken a hundred times before, past the gully where once we found a dead sheep, past the place where we built a beacon for the Queen.

At the top, all the familiar landmarks were laid out clear – the Usk river shining in sinuous curves, the bold tent-shape of the Blorenge mountain silhouetted against the sky, Skirrid Fawr with its humped back, Skirrid Fach marking the boundary of my uncle's farmland. I cast my mother's ashes into the wind and waited silently as they whirled out over the glittering valley.

NOTES

BEGINNING

1 William Cobbett, *Rural Rides* (London, 1830), Burghclere,
31 October 1825.
2 W. T. Palmer, 'Unveiling the War Memorial Tablet, Great
Gable, June 8th, 1924' in the *Journal of the Fell and Rock
Climbing Club of the English Lake District*, vol. 6, 1922–4.
Accessed via www.frcc.co.uk archive.

Chapter 1: LOOKING AT THE LAKES

1 Joseph Warton, *An Essay on the Genius and Writings of Pope*
(London, 1756).
2 Edmund Burke, *Philosophical Enquiry into the Origin of our Ideas
of the Sublime and the Beautiful* (London, 1757).
3 William Wordsworth, letter to the editor of the *Morning Post*,
9 December 1844, reprinted in William Wordsworth, *Guide to
the Lakes*, 1835 (London, 2004).
4 *Spectator*, no. 859, 14 December 1844.
5 William Hutchinson, *An Excursion to the Lakes in Westmoreland
and Cumberland, August 1773* (London, 1774).
6 Malcolm Andrews, *The Search for the Picturesque* (Aldershot,
1989).
7 Thomas Gray's journal in Thomas West, *A Guide to the Lakes, in
Cumberland, Westmorland, and Lancashire*, 2nd edn (London,
1780).
8 Thomas Gray, Letter to Joseph Warton, 1 October 1769,
quoted in Paget Toynbee and Leonard Whibley (eds),
Correspondence of Thomas Gray (Oxford, 1935).

9 William Wordsworth, *The Prelude*, Book XI (Harmondsworth, 1971).

10 John Keats, *Selected Poems and Letters* (London, 1995).

11 Robert Southey, *Letters from England* (London, 1807).

12 Samuel Taylor Coleridge, Ullswater, November 1799, in Kathleen Coburn (ed.), *The Notebooks of Samuel Taylor Coleridge 1794–1804*, vol. I (London, 1957).

13 *Ryaal Water* is at the Victoria and Albert Museum; *View at Ambleside* is at Tate Britain.

Chapter 2: PAINTING THE PROSPECT

1 Thomas Blount, *Glossographia* (London, 1656).

2 *The Complete Oxford English Dictionary*, 2nd edn (Oxford, 1989).

3 Ibid.

4 Review of an exhibition of works by Hogarth, Gainsborough and Wilson held at the British Institute for Promoting the Fine Arts in the United Kingdom, May–August 1814, quoted in Thomas Wright, *Some Account of the Life of Richard Wilson, Esq., R.A.* (London, 1824).

5 Henry Fuseli, *Lectures on Painting* (London, 1801).

6 Prince Hoare, *Epochs of the Arts* (London, 1813).

7 Now in The Barber Institute of Fine Arts, University of Birmingham.

8 Mary Woodall, *The Letters of Thomas Gainsborough* (London, 1963).

9 For a full account of the journey see Peter Hughes, 'Paul Sandby and Sir Watkin Williams-Wynn' in *The Burlington Magazine*, vol. 114, no. 832 (July 1972).

10 Quoted in W. T. Whitley, *Artists and their Friends in England 1700–1799* (London, 1928).

11 Edmund Burke, *A Philosophical Enquiry into the Origin of our Ideas of the Sublime and the Beautiful* (London, 1757).

12 James Usher, *Clio; or a discourse on taste* (London, 1769).

13 William Gilpin, *Three Essays: On Picturesque Beauty; On Picturesque Travel; and on Sketching Landscape* (London, 1792).

14 William Gilpin, *An Essay upon Prints* (London, 1768).

15 Now in the Bodleian Library, Oxford.
16 The correspondence between William Gilpin and William
   Mason is quoted in Carl Paul Barbier, *William Gilpin: His
   Drawings, Teaching, and Theory of the Picturesque* (Oxford, 1963).
17 William Gilpin, *Observations on the River Wye* (London, 1782).
18 Ibid.
19 Ibid.
20 Ibid.
21 William Gilpin quoted in John Hayes, *Richard Wilson* (Paulton,
   1966).
22 Gilpin, *Observations*.
23 Ibid.
24 Ibid.
25 The Hon. John Byng, 'Tour to the West 1781' in C. Bruyn
   Andrews (ed.), *The Torrington Diaries* (London, 1934).
26 Geoffrey Grigson, *Samuel Palmer* (London, 1947).

Chapter 3: A FITTING LANDSCAPE

1 The plea to Agitius, first found in Gildas's *De Excidio et
   Conquestu Britanniae* (sixth century), was later repeated in
   Bede's *Historia ecclesiastica gentis Anglorum* (731). P. H. Sawyer,
   From Roman Britain to Norman England (London, 2002).
2 Joseph Addison, writing in the *Spectator*, no. 412 (June, 1712).
3 Hugh Blair, *Lectures on rhetoric and belles lettres* (Dublin, 1783).
4 James Beattie, *Dissertations moral and critical* (London, 1783).
5 Celia Fiennes, *Through England on a Side Saddle in the Time of
   William and Mary, Being the Diary of Celia Fiennes* (London,
   1888), accessible via http://www.visionofbritain.org.uk.
6 Daniel Defoe, *Tour thro' the whole island of Great Britain*
   (London, 1724–7).
7 Richard Wilson, quoted in Geoffrey Grigson, *Britain Observed*
   (London, 1975).
8 John Constable, writing to Archdeacon John Fisher,
   23 October 1821, in R. B. Beckett (ed.), *John Constable's
   Correspondence*, vol. VI (Ipswich, 1968).

Chapter 4: 'I SHOULD PAINT MY OWN PLACES BEST'

1 Quoted in Martin Hardie, *Watercolour Painting in Britain*, vol. II (London, 1967).
2 William Wordsworth, 'Ode', 1816, *Miscellaneous Poems* (London, 1820).
3 John Constable's correspondence has been published in several volumes by the Suffolk Records Society. The letters to Archdeacon John Fisher that are quoted in this chapter appear in R. B. Beckett (ed.), *John Constable's Correspondence*, vol. VI (Ipswich, 1968).
4 C. R. Leslie, *Memoirs of the Life of John Constable RA*, 2nd edn (London, 1845).
5 Solomon Hart, *Reminiscences* (London, 1882).
6 John Eagles, quoted in W. T. Whitley, *Artists and their Friends in England 1700–1799* (London, 1928).
7 John Constable, *Various Subjects of Landscape* (London, 1833), included in R. B. Beckett, ed., *John Constable's Discourses* (Ipswich, 1970).
8 Ibid.
9 Constable's commentaries on the mezzotints included in *Various Subjects of Landscape* accompany the list of engravings.
10 'East Bergholt, Suffolk' from Constable's list of engravings in *Various Subjects of Landscape*, included in *John Constable's Discourses*, compiled and edited by R. B. Beckett (Suffolk Records Society, 1970).
11 John Constable, Lecture IV, 'The Decline and Revival of Landscape', *John Constable's Discourses*.
12 Henry Fuseli, *Lectures on painting* (London, 1801).
13 Martin Postle and Robin Simon (eds), *Richard Wilson and the Transformation of European Landscape Painting* (New Haven, CT and London, 2014).

Chapter 5: THE HIGHLANDS

1 Dorothy Wordsworth, 'A Tour made in Scotland (AD 1803)' in E. de Selincourt, ed., *The Journals of Dorothy Wordsworth* (London, 1941).

2 William Gilpin, *Observations, relative chiefly to Picturesque Beauty, Made in the Year 1776, on Several Parts of Great Britain; particularly the High-Lands of Scotland* (London, 1789).

3 Paget Toynbee and Leonard Whibley, eds, *Correspondence of Thomas Gray* (Oxford, 1935).

4 Benjamin Heath Malkin, *The Scenery, Antiquities and Biography of South Wales* (London, 1807).

5 Unnamed source quoted in James Holloway, *The Discovery of Scotland* (Edinburgh, 1978).

6 Turner, prospectus to *Liber Studiorum*, a series of landscapes and seascapes published as etchings and mezzotints between c. 1806 and 1824.

7 Joseph Mallord William Turner's *The Falls of the Clyde* (c. 1840) is held at Lady Lever Art Gallery, Port Sunlight, Liverpool.

Chapter 6: MAKING THE JOURNEY

1 Arthur Young, *A Six Weeks' Tour Through the Southern Counties of England and Wales* (London, 1768).

2 *Cornelius Varley's Narrative Written by Himself* appears in the catalogue of an exhibition of Varley's drawings and watercolours held at Colnaghi's Gallery, London, 21 February–16 March 1973.

Chapter 7: HEAVENLY HAFOD

1 Henry Penruddocke Wyndham, *A Tour through Monmouthshire and Wales*, 2nd edn (Salisbury, 1781).

2 Benjamin Heath Malkin, *The Scenery, Antiquities, and Biography of South Wales* (London, 1807).

3 James Edward Smith, *Fifteen Views Illustrative of a Tour to Hafod in Cardiganshire* (London, 1810).

4 They are now in the National Museum of Wales at Cardiff.

5 For a full discussion of this possibility, see Caroline Kerkham, *RSA Journal* vol. 139, no. 5413, December 1990.

6 George Cumberland, *An Attempt to Describe Hafod* (1796); a facsimile edition, edited by Jennifer Macve and Andrew Sclater, was published for the Bicentenary by the Hafod Trust (Ceredigion, 1996).

7 John Clark, *A General View of the Agriculture of the County of Hereford* (London, 1794).

8 Thomas Johnes, *A Cardiganshire Landlord's Advice to his Tenants* (Bristol, 1800).

9 Quoted in Elisabeth Inglis-Jones, *Peacocks in Paradise* (London, 1950).

Chapter 8: THE BOARD OF AGRICULTURE

1 Quoted in the entry on Arthur Young in the *Oxford Dictionary of National Biography* (online edition, September 2013).

2 Abraham and William Driver, *General View of the Agriculture of the County of Hampshire* (London, 1794).

3 James Donaldson, *General View of the Agriculture of the County of Northampton* (London, 1794).

4 Thomas Lloyd and Revd Mr Turnor, *General View of the Agriculture of the County of Cardigan* (London, 1794).

5 Ibid.

6 Ibid.

7 Contained in George Kay, *General View of the Agriculture of North Wales* (Edinburgh, 1794).

8 Ibid.

9 George Kay, in an open letter accompanying his *General View*.

10 George Kay on Penmaenmawr, ibid.

11 Joseph Hucks, *Pedestrian Tour Through North Wales* (London, 1795).

12 Charles Hassall, *General View of the Agriculture of the County of Carmarthenshire* (London, 1794).

13 John Bailey and George Culley, *General View of the Agriculture of the County of Cumberland* (London, 1794).

14 Sir Ernest Clarke, *History of the Board of Agriculture 1793–1822*
(London, 1898).
15 John Holt, *General View of the Agriculture of the County of Lancaster*
(London, 1795).
16 William Marshall, *The Rural Economy of the West of England*
(London, 1796).

Chapter 9: WILLIAM COBBETT

Cobbett's 'Rural Rides' were first published as articles in the *Political Register*, the journal that Cobbett founded in January 1802 and which continued until his death in June 1835. The rides started to appear in the *Political Register* from 1821 onwards. The first edition of the collected rides, *Rural Rides*, was published in 1830. The edition quoted is the one edited by G. D. H. and Margaret Coles in 1930. Cobbett's rides take in detailed itineraries; for brevity I have given just the place and date that the journal entries were made.

1 William Cobbett, *Rural Rides* (London, 1830), edited by
G.D.H. and Margaret Cole (London, 1930); this note was
taken at Foot's Cray 28 July 1825.
2 Ibid., Horsham, 31 July 1823.
3 Ibid., Elverton Farm, near Faversham, Kent, 4 December 1821.
4 These notes were taken at Cirencester, 7 Novermber 1821 and
Gloucester, 8 November 1821, on Cobbett's first ride.
5 William Cobbett, quoted in H. J. Massingham, *The Wisdom of
the Fields* (London, 1945).
6 Cobbett, *Rural Rides*, Burghclere, 20 November 1821.
7 Cobbett, *Political Register*, 5 May 1821.
8 William Hazlitt, *The Spirit of the Age,* 2nd edn (London, 1825).
9 Mary Russell Mitford, *Recollections of a Literary Life* (London, 1852).
10 Cobbett, *Political Register*, 14 December 1822.
11 Cobbett, *Rural Rides*, Reigate, 20 October 1825.
12 Ibid., Petersfield, 11 November 1825.
13 Ibid., Westerham, 6 September 1823.
14 Ibid., Canterbury, 4 September 1823.

15 Ibid., Kensington, 4 January 1822.

16 Ibid., Huntingdon, 22 January 1822.

17 Ibid., Kensington, 24 June 1822.

18 Ibid., Canterbury, 4 September 1823.

19 Ibid., Thursley, Surrey, 7 August 1823.

20 Ibid., Burghclere, 31 October 1825.

Chapter 10: OF ROOKS AND SHEEP

1 See *Sun,Wind and Rain*, held in the Birmingham Museum and Art Galleries.

2 Gilbert White, letter to Hon. Daines Barrington (letter CIII, undated), in Revd. Gilbert White, *The Natural History of Selborne* (London, 1789).

3 William Turner of Oxford, *Stonehenge – A Showery Day*, now held in the Ashmolean Museum, University of Oxford.

4 William Cobbett, *Rural Rides*, 1830 (London, 1930): Salisbury, 30 August 1826.

5 John Claridge, *General View of the Agriculture in the County of Dorset* (London, 1793).

Chapter 11: COMMON LAND

1 The Common Land Forum's report, 1986, accessed via publications.naturalengland.co.uk/publications216081. The record was published on 1 July 1986.

2 Memorandum to the Environment, Food and Rural Affairs Select Committee: Post-Legislative Assessment of the Commons Act 2006, February 2013. Accessed online via https://www.gov.uk/government/uploads/system/uploads/attachment_data/file/235960/8551.pdf

Chapter 12: LANDSCAPE AND FARMERS

1 The Anglo-Saxon Chronicle was a collection of reports in Old English originally gathered together in the ninth century AD,

probably in Wessex. Quoted in Caroline and Frank Thorn (eds), *Domesday Book: Dorset* (Chichester, 1983).

2 Ibid.

3 Owen Paterson, 'Keeping the Lights On', the 2014 Annual Global Warming Policy Foundation lecture, delivered 15 October 2014, published online at www.thegwpf.org.

4 William Wordsworth, *A Guide Through the District of the Lakes*, 1835 (London, 2004).

Chapter 13: DRESSING THE SKELETON

1 Margaret Gelling, *Place-Names in the Landscape* (London, 1984).

2 Quoted by W. G. Hoskins in *The Making of the English Landscape* (London, 1955).

3 Geoffrey King, *Observations and Conclusions upon the State and Condition of England*, 1696, accessed via www.york.ac.uk/depts/mahs/histat/king.htm)

4 William Marshall, *Rural Economy of Norfolk* (London, 1787).

5 Anne Tibble, ed., *John Clare. The Journals, Essays and the Journey from Essex* (Manchester, 1980).

6 John Holt, *General View of the Agriculture of the County of Lancaster* (London, 1795).

7 Ibid.

8 Ibid.

9 Uvedale Price, *Essays on the Picturesque* (London, 1810).

10 Charles Dickens, *Hard Times* (London, 1854).

11 W. G. Hoskins, *The Making of the English Landscape* (London, 1955).

12 Ibid.

Chapter 14: A PARTICULAR PATCH

1 Thomas Hardy, *The Return of the Native*, 1878 (London, 1964).

2 R. S. Thomas, 'The Small Window' in R. S. Thomas, *Collected Poems* (London, 2012).

3 There are 120,000 miles of footpaths and bridleways in England alone.

4 Henry Mayhew, *London Labour and the London Poor*, 1851 (Oxford, 2012).

Chapter 15: THOMAS HARDY'S WESSEX

1 Entry dated 20 January 1947 in James Lees Milne, *Caves of Ice* (London, 1983).

2 John Fowles, *Thomas Hardy's England* (London, 1989).

3 Hardy married his first wife, Emma Gifford, in 1874, but they subsequently became estranged. She died in 1912 and Hardy then married his secretary, Florence Dugdale. But he left instructions that, on his own death, his body was to be buried in the same grave as his first wife. His executor, Sydney Cockerell, thought that Poets' Corner in Westminster Abbey would be a more suitable resting place. So a bizarre compromise was reached, whereby Hardy's heart was buried in Emma Gifford's grave at Stinsford church near Dorchester, while his ashes went to Poets' Corner.

4 For a fuller account see J. H. Bettey, 'The Arnold Family of Ilsington' in *Notes and Queries for Somerset and Dorset*, vol. XXXVII, September 2011, Part 374.

5 John Claridge, *General View of the Agriculture in the County of Dorset* (London, 1793).

6 Hadrian Cook and Tom Williamson (eds), *Water Management in the English Landscape* (Edinburgh, 1999).

7 Thomas Hardy, *The Return of the Native*, 1878 (London, 1964).

8 Thomas Hardy, *The Woodlanders*, 1887 (London, 1964).

9 Thomas Hardy, *Far from the Madding Crowd*, 1874 (London, 1962).

10 Hardy, *Woodlanders*.

Chapter 16: WHAT DOES LANDSCAPE OFFER?

1 *The Complete Oxford English Dictionary*, 2nd edn (Oxford, 1989).

2 Johnson Grant, 'A London Journal of a Three Weeks Tour, in 1797, through Derbyshire to the Lakes', quoted in Malcolm Andrews, *The Search for the Picturesque* (Aldershot, 1989).

3 R. S. Thomas, 'The Bright Field', in R. S. Thomas, *Collected Poems* (London, 1993).

4 Quoted from A. H. Palmer, *Life and Letters of Samuel Palmer* (Cambridge, 2010).

BIBLIOGRAPHY

Andrews, C. Bruyn (ed.), *The Torrington Diaries* (London, 1934)

Andrews, Malcolm, *The Search for the Picturesque* (Aldershot, 1989)

Ashfield, Andrew and de Bolla, Peter, *The Sublime: A Reader in British Eighteenth-Century Aesthetic Theory* (Cambridge, 1996)

Bailey, J. and Culley, G., *General View of the Agriculture of the County of Cumberland* (London, 1794)

Barbier, Carl Paul, *William Gilpin: His Drawings, Teaching, and Theory of the Picturesque* (Oxford, 1963)

Barrell, John, *The Idea of Landscape and the Sense of Place* (Cambridge, 1972)

Beattie, James, *Dissertations moral and critical* (London, 1783)

Beckett, R. B. (ed.), *John Constable's Correspondence* (Ipswich, 1968)

Beckett, R.B. (ed.), *John Constable's Discourses* (Ipswich, 1970)

Blair, Hugh, *Lectures on rhetoric and belles lettres* (Dublin, 1783)

Blount, Thomas, *Glossographia* (London, 1656)

Brennan, Matthew C., *Wordsworth, Turner and Romantic Landscape: A Study of the Traditions of the Picturesque and Sublime* (Columbia, SC, 1987)

Burke, Edmund, *A Philosophical Enquiry into the Origin of our Ideas of the Sublime and the Beautiful* (London, 1757)

Clare, John, *see* Tibble, Anne

Claridge, John, *General View of the Agriculture in the County of Dorset* (London, 1793)

Clark, John, *General View of the Agriculture of the County of Hereford* (London, 1794)

Clark, Kenneth, *Landscape into Art* (London, 1949)

Clarke, Sir Ernest, *History of the Board of Agriculture 1793–1822* (London, 1898)

Cobbett, William, *Rural Rides* (London, 1830), edited by G.D.H. and Margaret Cole (London, 1930)

Coburn, Kathleen (ed.), *The Notebooks of Samuel Taylor Coleridge 1794–1804*, vol. 1 (London, 1957)

Constable, John, *see* Beckett, R. B.

Cook, Hadrian and Williamson, Tom (eds), *Water Management in the English Landscape* (Edinburgh, 1999)

Cumberland, George, *An Attempt to Describe Hafod*, facsimile of 1796 edition published by the Hafod Trust (Ceredigion, 1996)

Daniels, Stephen, *Fields of Vision: Landscape, Imagery and National Identity in England and the United States* (Princeton, NJ, 1993)

Davis, Thomas, *General View of Agriculture in the County of Wiltshire* (London, 1794)

Defoe, Daniel, *Tour thro' the whole island of Great Britain* (London 1724–7), edited by Pat Rodgers (Harmondsworth, 1978)

Donaldson, James, *General View of the Agriculture of the County of Northampton* (London, 1794)

Driver, Abraham and William, *General View of the Agriculture of the County of Hampshire* (London, 1794)

Fiennes, Miss Celia, *Through England on a Side Saddle in the Time of William and Mary, Being the Diary of Celia Fiennes* (London, 1888). Accessible via http://www.visionofbritain.org.uk.

Fuseli, Henry, *Lectures on Painting: delivered at the Royal Academy* (London, 1801)

Gelling, Margaret, *Place-Names in the Landscape* (London, 1984)

Gerard, Thomas, *Survey of Dorsetshire (c.1630)* reprinted by the Dorset Publishing Company (Wincanton, 1980)

Gilpin, William, *An Essay upon Prints* (London, 1768)

Gilpin, William, *Observations on the River Wye* (London, 1782)

Gilpin, William, *Observations, relative Chiefly to Picturesque Beauty, Made in the Year 1772, on Several Parts of England; Particularly the Mountains, and Lakes of Cumberland and Westmoreland* (London, 1786)

Gilpin, William, *Observations, relative chiefly to Picturesque Beauty, Made in the Year 1776, on Several Parts of Great Britain; particularly the High-Lands of Scotland* (London, 1789)

Gilpin, William, *Three Essays: On Picturesque Beauty; On Picturesque Travel; and on Sketching Landscape* (London, 1792)

Gilpin, William, *Observations on the Western Parts of England* (London, 1798)

Gilpin, William, *Observations on Several Parts of England* (London, 1808)

Gittings, Robert (ed.), *John Keats: Selected Poems and Letters* (London, 1995)

Gray, Thomas, *Odes* (London, 1757)

Grigson, Geoffrey, *Samuel Palmer* (London, 1947)

Grigson, Geoffrey, *Britain Observed* (London, 1975)

Hardy, Thomas, *Far from the Madding Crowd*, 1874 (London, 1962)

Hardy, Thomas, *The Return of the Native*, 1878 (London, 1964)

Hardy, Thomas, *The Woodlanders*, 1887 (London, 1964)

Hart, Solomon, *Reminiscences* (London, 1882)

Hassall, Charles, *General View of the Agriculture of the County of Carmarthen* (London, 1794)

Hawkes, Jacquetta, *A Land* (London, 1951)

Hayes, John, *Richard Wilson* (Paulton, 1966)

Hazlitt, William, *The Spirit of the Age*, 2nd edn (London, 1825)

Hoare, Prince, *Epochs of the Arts* (London, 1813)

Holloway, James, *The Discovery of Scotland: The appreciation of Scottish scenery through two centuries of painting* (Edinburgh, 1978)

Holt, John, *General View of the Agriculture of the County of Lancaster* (London, 1795)

Hoskins, W. G., *The Making of the English Landscape* (London, 1955)

Hoskins, W. G., *The Midland Peasant* (London, 1957)

Hoskins, W. G., *Provincial England* (London, 1963)

Hucks, John, *A Pedestrian Tour through North Wales* (London, 1795)

Hughes, Peter, 'Paul Sandby and Sir Watkin Williams-Wynn' in *The Burlington Magazine*, vol. 114, no. 832 (July 1972)

Humphreys, Richard, *The British Landscape* (London, 1989)

Hussey, Christopher, *The picturesque: studies in a point of view* (London, 1927)

Hutchinson, William, *An Excursion to the Lakes, in Westmoreland and Cumberland, August 1773* (London, 1774)

Inglis-Jones, Elisabeth, *Peacocks in Paradise* (London, 1950)

Kay, George, *General View of the Agriculture of North Wales* (Edinburgh, 1794)

Keats, John, *see* Gittings, Robert

King, Gregory, *Observations and Conclusions upon the State and Condition of England* (1696), accessed via www.york.ac.uk/depts/mahs/histstat/king.htm

Knight, Richard Payne, *The Landscape* (London, 1795)

Landscape in Britain 1850–1950 (Tate Gallery exhibition catalogue, 1983)

Leslie, C. R., *Memoirs of the Life of John Constable RA*, 2nd edn (London, 1845)

Lipscomb, George, *Journey into South Wales* (London, 1802)

Lloyd, Thomas and Revd Mr Turnor, *General View of the Agriculture of the County of Cardigan* (London, 1794)

Malkin, Benjamin Heath, *The Scenery, Antiquities and Biography of South Wales* (London, 1807)

Marshall, William, *Minutes of Agriculture* (London, 1778)

Marshall, William, *The Rural Economy of Norfolk*, 2 vols (London, 1787)

Marshall, William, *The Rural Economy of the Midland Counties* (London, 1790)

Marshall, William, *The Rural Economy of the West of England* (London, 1796)

Marshall, William, *A Review of the Reports to the Board of Agriculture from the Western Department* (York, 1808)

Marshall, William, *The Review and Abstracts of the County Reports to the Board of Agriculture*, reprint of 1818 edn (Newton Abbot, 1969)

Matless, David, *Landscape and Englishness* (London, 1998)

Mills, A. D., *The Place Names of Dorset: Part Four*, compiled by the English Place-Name Society (Nottingham, 2010)

Mitford, Mary Russell, *Recollections of a Literary Life* (London, 1852)

Morley, David, and Robins, Kevin (eds), *British Cultural Studies: Geography, Nationality and Identity* (Oxford, 2001)

Ousby, Ian, *The Englishman's England* (Cambridge, 1990)

Palmer, A. H., *Life and Letters of Samuel Palmer*, 1892 (Cambridge, 2010)

Parris, Leslie, *Landscape in Britain c. 1750–1850* (Tate Gallery exhibition catalogue, 1973)

Percival, Thomas, *Moral and literary dissertations*, in particular 'On the advantages of a taste for the general beauties of nature and art' (Warrington, 1774)

Pevsner, Nikolaus and Newman, John, *The Buildings of England: Dorset* (Harmondsworth, 1972)

Postle, Martin and Simon, Robin (eds), *Richard Wilson and the Transformation of European Landscape Painting* (London and New Haven, CT, 2014)

Price, Uvedale, *Essays on the Picturesque* (London, 1810)

Salvesen, Christopher, *The Landscape of Memory* (London, 1965)

Sawyer, P. H., *From Roman Britain to Norman England* (London, 2002)

Schama, Simon, *Landscape and Memory* (London, 1995)

de Selincourt, E. (ed.), *The Journals of Dorothy Wordsworth* (London, 1941)

Smith, James Edward, *Fifteen Views Illustrative of a Tour to Hafod in Cardiganshire* (London, 1810)

Southey, Robert, *Letters from England* (London, 1807)

Stevenson, W., *General View of the Agriculture of Dorset* (London, 1812)

Taylor, Christopher, *The Making of the English Landscape: Dorset* (London, 1970)

Thomas, R. S., *Collected Poems* (London, 1993)

Thomas, R. S., *Collected Poems* (London, 2012)

Thomson, James, *The Seasons* (Edinburgh, 1730)

Thorn, Caroline and Frank (eds), *Domesday Book: Dorset* (Chichester, 1983)

Tibble, Anne (ed.), *John Clare: The Journals, Essays and the Journey from Essex* (Manchester, 1980)

Toynbee, Paget and Whibley, Leonard (eds), *Correspondence of Thomas Gray* (Oxford, 1935)

Usher, James, *Clio; or a discourse on taste* (London, 1769)

Varley, Cornelius, *Cornelius Varley's Narrative Written by Himself*, in the catalogue of the exhibition of Varley's prints and drawings at Colnaghi's Gallery (London, 1973)

Warton, Joseph, *An Essay on the Genius and Writings of Pope* (London, 1756)

West, Thomas, *Guide to the Lakes, in Cumberland, Westmorland, and Lancashire* (London, 1778)

White, Revd Gilbert, *The Natural History of Selborne* (London, 1789)

Whitley, W. T., *Artists and their Friends in England 1700–1799* (London, 1928).

Wilcox, Scott, *Sun, Wind, and Rain: The Art of David Cox* (New Haven, CT, 2008)

Wilkinson, Joseph, *Select Views in Cumberland, Westmorland and Lancashire* (London, 1810)

Williams, Raymond, *Border Country* (London, 1960)

Wollstonecraft, Mary, *Posthumous works*, in particular 'On poetry and our relish for the beauties of nature' (London, 1798)

Woodall, Mary, *The Letters of Thomas Gainsborough* (London, 1963)

Wordsworth, William, *The Prelude* (Harmondsworth, 1971)

Wordsworth, William, *Poetry and Prose* (Oxford, 1956)

Wordsworth, William, *Guide to the Lakes, 1835* (London, 2004)

Wright, Thomas, *Some Account of the Life of Richard Wilson, Esq., R.A.* (London, 1824)

Wyndham, Henry P., *A Tour through Monmouthshire and Wales*, 2nd edn (Salisbury, 1781)

Yeates, G. K., *The Life of the Rook* (London, 1934)

Young, Arthur, *A Six Weeks' Tour Through the Southern Counties of England and Wales* (London, 1768)

Young, Arthur, *A Six Months' Tour Through the North of England*, 4 vols (London, 1770)

ACKNOWLEDGEMENTS

Writers, through their agents, generally seek a contract for a book that they are hoping to write. If they are successful in this, then the publisher knows roughly what to expect and when to expect it. But I'd written the whole of *Landskipping* before I dropped off the manuscript with my agent, Caradoc King at A. P. Watt. He was the first person to see it and I am hugely grateful to him and to Michael Fishwick at Bloomsbury for taking on with such zest a book that neither knew I was writing.

Michael Fishwick, the Publishing Director at Bloomsbury, delivered an exceptionally thoughtful commentary on the text, along with an airy flock of commas, which gave much-needed clarity. I am greatly indebted to him and his assistant Marigold Atkey. Once again, Victoria Millar has been a superb editor. I have been lucky enough to work with her before and was not surprised to find her as tenacious as ever in pursuit of a footnote. I am conscious of a great debt to her, and the book has benefitted immeasurably from her interventions. With great finesse, Anna Simpson guided the book through the production process. My grateful thanks go to her and to the designer Emma Ewbank. Catherine Best read the proofs and David Atkinson compiled the index.

Most of this book has been written in a cottage in Wester Ross where I have been going for a number of years. I would like to thank Ewen and Nicky Macpherson of Attadale for their unfailing kindness and hospitality. Colin Hamilton, of

Perthshire, is the only person to whom I have talked about my book during the long process of writing it. As ever, I have greatly valued his wise counsel. And his encouragement.

In Dorset, Philip Crawford kindly shared his expertise on matters to do with farming. While occupied in research for his own book, Tim Connor found in the archives material (such as the inventory quoted Chapter 14) which was extraordinarily useful for my own work and I appreciate, very much, his generosity in passing these plums on to me.

When I first started thinking about this project, I commissioned George Wright, a photographer with whom I've worked many times, to photograph one particular view throughout one whole year. The aim was to try and fix the way that a single landscape changes with the seasons and the time of day. He produced a superb sequence of images, which subsequently made it possible for me to write the penultimate chapter of this book.

My final thanks go to my husband, Trevor Ware, particularly for the food parcels – avocados, chocolate brownies – which he sent up to Wester Ross to help with the writing. They did.

LIST OF ILLUSTRATIONS

INDEX

A NOTE ON THE AUTHOR

Anna Pavord's books include her bestseller *The Tulip*, *The Naming of Names* and her most recent work, *The Curious Gardener*. Her column in the *Independent* newspaper has appeared ever since the paper was launched in 1986. She writes and presents programmes for BBC Radio 3 and 4 and served for ten years on the Gardens Panel of the National Trust, the last five as Chairman. For the last forty years she has lived in Dorset, England.

A NOTE ON THE TYPE

The text of this book is set in Perpetua. This typeface is an adaptation of a style of letter that had been popularised for monumental work in stone by Eric Gill. Large scale drawings by Gill were given to Charles Malin, a Parisian punch-cutter, and his hand-cut punches were the basis for the font issued by Monotype. First used in a private translation called 'The Passion of Perpetua and Felicity', the italic was originally called Felicity.